# *Owning Our Ovaries*
## Unleashing The Power Within

© 2025 Dawn Bates
Published by DBI Publishing
www.dawnbates.com

The moral rights of the authors have been asserted.

For quantity sales or media enquiries, please get in touch with the publisher at the website address above.

Cataloguing-in-Publication entry is available from the British Library.

ISBN:
978-1-9194007-1-6 (paperback)
978-1-9194007-2-3 (hardback)
978-1-9194007-0-9 (eBook)

Book cover design: Amanda Denham and Jerry Lampson
Developmental editor: Dawn Bates

1st Edition 2025 All rights reserved.

No part of this book may be reproduced, stored in a retrieval system, communicated, or transmitted in any form or by any means without written permission. All inquiries should be made to the publisher at the above address.

Disclaimer: The material in this publication is of the nature of general comment only and does not represent professional advice. It is not intended to provide specific guidance for individual circumstances and should not be relied upon as the basis for any decision to act or not to act on any matters it covers.

The opinions expressed in this publication are those of the contributors and do not reflect the opinions of the co-authors, DBI Publishing,

Dawn Bates International Ltd, or the editors. Information contained in this book has been obtained by the authors, DBI Publishing, and Dawn Bates International Ltd, from sources believed to be reliable.

However, neither the authors, editors, DBI Publishing, Dawn Bates International Ltd, guarantees the accuracy or completeness of any information published herein, and neither the authors, editors, DBI Publishing, Dawn Bates International Ltd shall be responsible for any errors, omissions, or claims for damages, including exemplary damages, arising out of use, inability to use, or concerning the accuracy or sufficiency of the information contained within.

Neither the editor, authors, publisher, nor any other party associated with the production of this book accepts responsibility for any accident or injury resulting from reading the content contained herein. Any individual choosing to select, purchase, and read this book does so at their own risk and must take full responsibility for their own choices, health, and well-being.

# ALSO PUBLISHED BY DBI PUBLISHING

## The Relentless Rebel Duology by Dawn Bates

Friday Bridge - Becoming a Muslim; Becoming Everyone's Business (1st Edition, 2013; 2nd Edition, 2017; 3rd Edition, 2023)

Walaahi - A Firsthand Account of Living Through the Egyptian Uprising and Why I Walked Away from Islaam (1st Edition, 2017; 2nd Edition, 2023)

## The Scotland Saga by Dawn Bates

Crossing the Line - A Journey of Purpose and Self-Belief (2018)

## The Sacral Series by Dawn Bates

Moana - One Woman's Journey Back to Self (2020)

Leila - A Life Renewed One Canvas at a Time (2020)

Pandora - Melting the Ice One Dive at a Time (2021)

Alpha - Saving Humanity One Vagina at a Time (2021)

Faith - Leaving Religion to Save Your Soul (2024)

## Anthologies

Break Down to Wake Up - Journey Beyond the Now, by Jocelyn Bellows (2020)

Standing in Strength - Inspirational Stories of Power Unleashed, by Laarni Mulvey (2021)

The Potent Power of Menopause - A Culturally Diverse Perspective of Feminine Transformation, by Dawn Bates and Clarissa Kristjansson (2022)

Alive to Thrive - Life After Attempting Suicide: Our Stories, by Dawn Bates and Debbie Debonaire (2022)

#ManUp, Tough to Talk, by Steve Whittle (2024)

## Memoirs/Biographies

Crossing the Line - A Journey of Purpose and Self-Belief, by Dawn Bates (2017)

Becoming Annie - The Biography of a Curious Woman, by Dawn Bates (2020)

Becoming the Champion - Volume 1: The Awareness, by Korey Carpenter (2020)

Unlocked - Discover Your Hidden Keys, by Carmelle Crinnion (2020)

The Recipe - A US Marine's Mindset for Success, by Jake Cosme (2021)

## Personal Development

51 Powerful Ps of Public Speaking, by Krystylle L. Richardson (2022)

## Fiction Books

Sin Eater - Memories Vanish When She Arrives, by Amanda Denham (2024)

Seven Feathers: There Is More Life After Death by Amanda Denham (2025)

Estella: A Novel by Lara Latcham (2025)

### The Democ-Chu Series by Nath Brye

Slave Boy (2020)

Blood Child (2021)

Slave Alone (2025)

To discover the latest books from DBI Publishing, please visit https://dawnbates.com/readers

*Dedicated to all the women who have fought and died over the decades, centuries and millennia, making the opportunities women of today have possible. May we honour your efforts and your legacy, building on it with respect, grace and fortitude.*

# Foreword

"You've got a big pair of balls for a woman," a comment made by a man after I challenged him at a business networking meeting, completely unaware of who he was or his standing in the community.
My response?
"Yep, they are called ovaries, and they are more powerful than a pair of testes will ever be, and more precious. That is why they are protected deep inside of me."
He loved the comeback and became one of my biggest champions in business, until I refused to have an affair with him behind both our spouses' backs. Then his support for me vanished in a heartbeat for all to notice.
Ever since the dawn of man, women have been an enigma to men, and exhibiting our personal power often results in devastating results for women. If we refuse a man, more often than not, our reputations are damaged in one way or another.
We have been beaten, abused, sexually assaulted, experimented on, dismissed, and ridiculed to such an extent that the psychological and physical damage has been passed down to their daughters and their sons for generations.
With the advent of publications, storytelling through films and music videos, and the more recent tool of social media, the psychological damage has increased, along with the awareness and bravery of a few women coming forward to say "No more." And sadly, in reality, it is a few.

Some women like the idea of stepping up to prevent the spreading of damaging behaviours, belief systems, and attitudes, but when it comes down to making those tough decisions, celebrating themselves, and removing the deeply buried shackles of life imposed, the majority still prefer to believe the bad narratives about themselves.

With a drive towards equity and inclusion, we have seen a growing number of women own their ovaries to embrace the potent power within themselves, only to fall back in line when things get tough. Why do they do this? Mainly because they are the solo carers of their children and cannot afford to lose everything they have worked hard for, whether it is their job, their home, their freedom, the children, or all of the above.

When it comes to sexual assault and rape, the Crime Survey for England and Wales (CSEW) estimated that 1.1 million adults aged sixteen and over experienced sexual assault in the year ending March 2022, with 798,000 women and 275,000 men affected. This equates to a prevalence rate of approximately 2.3 per cent of adults: 3.3 per cent women and 1.2 per cent men. Now imagine the figures were reversed, with three times as many men being raped. What do you think the lawmakers and governments would do then?

When we look at the figures for male suicide, which are just over three times the amount of women, we start seeing charities, men's groups, and wellbeing policies within corporations start happening in abundance. Women have been asking for help and support with menopause symptoms for decades, and yet it is only now that women are getting the support and resources they need, and at a huge personal cost - financially, emotionally, mentally and physically.

It is no secret that things start to change quite rapidly when the problems impact men, so why do we women keep allowing it to happen? Does it happen because men have more free time because they are not caring for children and parents as much as women? Or do women not rally together as much due to the social isolation, exhaustion, and depression caused by working both outside and inside the home?

When single dads cried out for support to see their kids due to the mother being favoured in divorce courts, we saw the Fathers For Justice campaign receive the media attention it deserved. And yet when single mums cry out for financial support and childcare facilities at or near work, what do we see? Not much. Not even the Child Maintenance

Service has much luck in getting dads to pay for the child they created. Female investors are few and far between, and rather than join forces nationally, most women set up little groups locally - then moan they don't get the support nationally they need. Collaboration is key, and men show this abundantly.

When it comes to managing their finances and being financially literate, women are closing the gap at 58 per cent compared to 72 per cent for men, but that is still only about half the female population with financial literacy. The reasons for this are unclear, but speak with any single mum and she will tell you she had no choice but to get good with finances. Some may argue that men leaving the mother with the children has been a blessing in disguise because the women are proving themselves to be strong, competent, and resourceful, but at what cost? According to a research paper by Linda A. Liang, Ursula Berger, and Christian Brand, *Psychosocial Factors Associated With Symptoms Of Depression, Anxiety and Stress Among Single Mothers With Young Children: A Population-Based Study*, approximately 30 per cent of single mothers reported experiencing depressive or anxiety symptoms and 37 per cent regularly experienced general stress. This is twice as high compared with partnered mothers. Parenting stress was also elevated, and the adjusted regression models confirmed that single mothers are twice as likely to report symptoms of depression or anxiety. With these findings, is it any wonder that the children of single-parent families struggle in school, have fewer opportunities in life, and require more safeguarding to protect them from external influences which could cause significant harm, possibly incarceration?

With women choosing to own their ovaries and take back control of their lives, their income levels, and their confidence, we are seeing women take their careers to even greater heights than ever before. Women in senior management and director roles have risen from 32 per cent in 2015 to 37 per cent in 2024, although these statistics are still racially biased towards white women. The Global Entrepreneurship Monitor also reported female established business ownership rates rising from 4.2 per cent in 2001-2005 to 5.9 per cent in 2021-2023, which is still fewer than six women for every one hundred men.

More women are accepting the narrative that they are less than men, a story many young girls have believed. Throughout history, women have stood in their power, refused to be beaten, hunted down, or imprisoned for refusing to comply with the laws, systems, and social etiquette men put in place. When they said it is a man's world, they were not joking. Today, we face new challenges. Men are increasingly being accepted as women in female-only spaces, jeopardising the sacred protections these spaces have historically provided. A striking example is the Giggle versus Tickle case in Australia. Sal Grover, a fierce defender of women's and girls' rights, fought to protect female-only spaces against the intrusion of men claiming to be women. Her courage has highlighted the very real dangers of accepting men as women in spaces meant exclusively for women, from safeguarding girls to preserving the physical and psychological safety of all women. This fight is not just about policy; it is about recognising the power, identity, and autonomy of women and ensuring we do not erode the foundations laid by centuries of female struggle.

Now things are changing, not as fast as they need to, but they are changing. Women are speaking up, leaving abusive and controlling relationships, and starting their own businesses in record numbers.

Recently, at an awards dinner, I was among over two hundred and fifty women gathered to celebrate each other for being shortlisted for various awards. Our host commented, "We are laying the foundations for women that come after us," but she was wrong. We are not laying foundations; we are building on those already laid centuries ago by incredible women throughout history who fought and often died for the rights of others. Today, this includes the six remarkable women from around the world whose stories are shared in this book, women who are proving that courage, strength, and resilience are still alive. The question now is whether the women of today will show as much courage, strength, and resilience as those women from hundreds of years ago.

And yet, our bodies are still not our own. We continue to suffer at the hands of men, and sadly, many women continue to fuel negative narratives and inequalities through fear or reluctance to break free from generational shackles.

When I came up with the idea for this book, it was to be one of six books in the Life Transformation Series; three focusing on women, and three focusing on men. My initial brief was for groups of ten individuals to share their stories in each of the books. As any writer will tell you, once a book starts, the vision shifts and evolves. One of the books in the Life Transformation Series is *The Potent Power of Menopause: A Culturally Diverse Perspective of Feminine Transformation*, which involved ten women and one man. There were going to be ten women involved with this book, but due to divorce, ill-health and changes in direction, four women are now longer featured in the book. An additional woman was not willing to provide proof of the allegations made within her story, so she had to be removed, and the others who were invited from around the world were not brave enough to share their stories.

So within this book, you'll find seven women who came together, sharing their stories filled with insights, raw emotions, bravery and hope for all who read it. These ladies come from a range of cultural, generational, religious, and lifestyle perspectives. I have worked closely with each of these remarkable women who are contributing their stories, supporting them every step of the way to ensure their voices are heard with clarity and impact. Together, we have created healing by osmosis, and as with all anthologies from DBI Publishing, readers have been given a space where to share their thoughts, ideas and actions they intend to take, making this book truly theirs. My co-authors and I hope that this book will help all our readers work safely, share authentically, and effect real social change, starting within themselves.

This book is not about the authors themselves, although the stories are theirs to tell. The stories are shared to reach all those impacted by the subjects covered, including domestic abuse, alcoholism, parental abuse, endometriosis, miscarriage, marriage breakdown, rape, systemic failure, police corruption, drug abuse, co-dependency, grooming, peer pressure, and parenting.

Working with women who have experienced trauma is challenging, especially while processing one's own challenging experiences, yet there is immense healing and growth in the process. During the process of bringing this book to life, I have changed as a woman, faced the loss of a very dear friend and mentor, moved countries, won a court case where I was put on trial for being raped, and have been in the process of dealing with two further legal battles - all because I refuse to be bullied and manipulated. They say, "pick your battles," and whilst I let a lot of things slide, there are battles which deserve our attention, and our energy, because if we don't fight them, then others are subjected to the pain, suffering and abuse we go through.

The women in this book, in their own way, all said, "This stops with me", and they have stepped up in various ways to make sure they are part of the solution to the many problems women today face.

Whilst this book reflects part of the original vision I had, it has grown into something more profound and powerful than I imagined. Not everyone within these pages writes for a living, nor do they own businesses. We are all just women, making our way through life, choosing to give back hope, courage, and strength to others whilst we navigate the aftermath, the anniversaries, the continued traumas and life changes we are all going through. I am proud of what we have created together, and honoured to have been blessed with the guardianship of these stories.

We hope the following pages help you gain courage, hope, understanding, and empathy for yourself and others. If you find yourself deeply moved, triggered, or affected by the stories within this book, please do not hesitate to reach out to your local support groups, doctors, mental health professionals, or trusted organisations. You are not alone, and seeking help is a sign of strength, not weakness. Your well-being matters, and there are people and resources ready to listen, guide, and support you.

With love and gratitude to you all,

Dawn x

Crime Survey for England and Wales, Sexual Offences in England and Wales: Year Ending March 2022,
https://www.ons.gov.uk/peoplepopulationandcommunity/crimeandjustice

Samaritans, Suicide Statistics, https://www.samaritans.org/about-samaritans/research-policy/suicide-facts-and-figures/

Fathers For Justice, Campaign History, https://fathersforjustice.org/

OECD, Financial Literacy Survey, https://www.oecd.org/financial/education/

Liang, L.A., Berger, U., Brand, C., *Psychosocial Factors Associated With Symptoms Of Depression, Anxiety And Stress Among Single Mothers With Young Children: A Population-Based Study*, Journal of Affective Disorders, Volume 242, 2019.

Australian Bureau of Statistics, Women in Leadership Positions, https://www.abs.gov.au/statistics/people/people-and-communities/women-leadership-positions

Global Entrepreneurship Monitor, Female Entrepreneurship Report, https://www.gemconsortium.org/report/gem-2021-2022-global-report

The Guardian, "Sall Grover begins federal court appeal against Roxanne Tickle's gender discrimination case win", https://www.theguardian.com/australia-news/2025/aug/04/sall-grover-giggle-app-federal-court-appeal-against-roxanne-tickle-gender-discrimination-case-ntwnfb

# Contents

Foreword ---------------------------------------------------------------- ix

Choosing Me ------------------------------------------------------------- 1
Are You Better Yet? ---------------------------------------------------- 29
Nevil. ----------------------------------------------------------------- 59
Endo Life -------------------------------------------------------------- 83
Art Therapy ----------------------------------------------------------- 105
This Thing Called Life ------------------------------------------------ 125
Owning My Ovaries, Owning My Energy ----------------------------------- 145
In Closing ------------------------------------------------------------ 171

Book Club & Women's Networking Group Questions -------------------------- i
Journalling Prompts ---------------------------------------------------- iv
Gratitude ------------------------------------------------------------- vii
About the Publisher -------------------------------------------------- viii

Dawn Bates,
Britain... for now.

Dawn Bates is an author, publisher, and social justice advocate with a career spanning nearly 30 years across 47 countries.

As founder of Dawn Bates International, she has established herself as a leader in transformative storytelling, empowering authors to create works that influence cultural understanding and drive systemic change. Her own writing addresses some of the most challenging issues of our time, including systemic abuse, government corruption, religious diversity, and gender justice. In addition to her publishing and coaching work, Dawn hosts an international podcast, has written for many leading magazines in the personal development and business space, and is currently pursuing her PhD in Social Justice and Literary Activism.

Known for her honesty, humour, and cultural insight, Dawn offers audiences not only analysis but also lived experience, making her an authoritative and compelling voice on global citizenship, inclusion, and human rights.

To discover more about Dawn, please visit www.dawnbates.com
To connect with Dawn, please use https://linkedin.com/in/dawnbates

# Choosing Me

### Sailing the world.

Sitting on a luxury yacht anchored off the island of Efate, Vanuatu, tears fell from my eyes, having risen from the depths of my soul. These weren't just tears; these were the floodgates of my soul breaking open because I'd just made a choice that would impact my children and me for the rest of our lives.

Looking back now, I know it was the right choice, but in that moment, I felt like the choice I'd just made was the most selfish, irresponsible choice a mother could make.

Here I was in one of the most beautiful parts of the world, and I'd chosen to stay, rather than return home to my children. I just wasn't ready, and the thought of returning home to Sheffield, England, filled me with dread - even though the one constant desire in my entire life, the way I had designed and built my life, was to be the very best mum I could be. If I returned home to them now, I couldn't deliver on that promise to them-or myself.

From the moment my careers teacher at school told the class, "I want you to think of the one thing you want to become in life, and write that down". I wrote down, without hesitation, 'I want to be a mum' and I planned my entire life around being a full-time mum.

I set up my business so that no one could tell me, "No," when I wanted time off to care for my two boys, whom I knew would be born four years apart, before the age of thirty. This was years before I'd met the man I chose to marry and have children with. I chose an office big enough for my boys to have space just for them, their bassinet, and a changing table. With a fold-out double bed masquerading as an office couch, it was perfect if the team and I needed to pull an all-nighter to complete projects. It was also great for afternoon naps with the boys. The office was also next door to a private day nursery where, once they were old enough, the boys attended on a half-day basis.

When I hosted or attended business meetings, the boys would be with me, either asleep in their car seats or in a space within the meeting room close to me. I've breastfed my boys whilst sitting on expert panels in front of hundreds of people, had them hand out paper, pens, and gift bags when they were five years old. They've been around the world of business and adults all their lives, learning how to behave, how to conduct business meetings and ask relevant questions - absorbing all the wisdom and success energy in the room.

I knew from the depths of my soul that I did not want daughters. That idea filled me with dread. Boys, on the other hand, excited me on every level. When the boys arrived, they became the centre of my life, and not in the mummy martyr or toxic co-dependent way either. No, my boys were raised as strong, interdependent men, capable of taking care of themselves and their families when they grew up, and they would be strong in mind, body, and spirit.

Setting firm foundations within the first eleven and fifteen years of their lives, I'd done with every vibration of my soul. Now, it was time for their father to step up and lead them his way, without me there to interfere or second-guess his choices. Ultimately, giving him space to parent the way he wanted to. I'd chosen him to be their father, believing he'd be a great dad. Now it was his time to shine.

## In the beginning.

"I may love you, but I don't like you very much", words my mother would say to me as I was growing up. I don't know how many times she said it, but it was often enough that I'd finish the sentence for her.

These words formed the backdrop of my internal narrative throughout my life, making me question why people were friends with me. Constant questioning of the motives of others, my siblings, school friends, boys who showed an interest, and even the man who'd become my husband. These words would also form the background narrative when it came to business. I didn't trust people when they said they liked me or that we were friends. Either I was paying them or they were paying me. It was transactional, because why would they like me? I was simply providing them with a service or a product, or paying them for one.

Growing up in an idyllic farming village with expansive skies, I'd stare off into the distance. I wondered why my mum didn't like me, especially when I was always so helpful with chores, quiet with my books, and would sing and dance with her in the kitchen. When she would get her piecemeal work, one of the three jobs she did to keep a roof over *my* head, not hers or my siblings - just mine, I'd be eager to help, often doing the work for her whilst she got the dinner ready.

Sometimes, I'd walk for miles or ride my bike, lie down in our garden with the dogs and stare at the clouds, filling in the empty spaces with wonder, seeing images of animals, land, and seascapes. Other times, I'd lie there with my arms outstretched and swear I could feel the earth spinning so fast with me. I came to love the feeling of just lying on the ground with my eyes closed. I felt peace and the incredible sense of belonging, something I never felt anywhere, except for the characters in my books or lost in the encyclopedias my mum had saved up for me to stop me from asking my endless questions about things she didn't know about.

I remember being bullied at school, bullied by my older brother, and bullied by the other kids in the village. I enjoyed school for the learning, not because I got to be or play with other kids, but because I got to learn so many new things.

With the ability to see for miles across the Fenland flat landscapes, or far out to sea, I would paint pictures in my mind of what appeared to others as nothingness. These blank spaces were like a canvas for me, filling them with places I wanted to visit, experiences and things I wanted to enjoy. It would set the tone for my future in ways I couldn't imagine.

Images, akin to jigsaw puzzle pieces, started to form in front of me. Images created from the shadows, the trees, and the hedgerows blended with the information I'd listen to in class each day. I'd see faces and imagery in food patterns, tree bark and pretty much anything that had different textures and depths to them.

Reading books, listening to music, and watching TV all helped me imagine even more than I could see around me. Connecting the dots of everything I was learning, I created imagery on top of imagery, knowing deep down that magic was happening. I didn't know quite what kind of magic, but I knew *something* was happening. I would smile, get goose bumps, and become excited about the world around me. That excited feeling when you almost squeeze yourself so tightly from the inside out, pulling your arms into you, fists clenched and a big, open-mouth smile on your face - yep, I was so excited only dogs could hear me.

Seeing silver raindrops float down in front of me, and with my younger sister telling me she couldn't see them, I felt even more magical. When people shone with different colours or looked 'funny' with a haze around them, my mum knew it was time to take me to the doctors. *"She says people look different colours, and she says she sees silver raindrops. What's wrong with her?"* I remember my mum asking more than one doctor before she was told, *"She is experiencing auras, quite common for girls in puberty"*. I remember my mum sitting there just looking at me, in one of her black jumpers with a cat on the front, not knowing quite what to say to me. Finally, she accepted I wasn't strange, or abnormal, or even crazy. I kept looking at her, wondering why she looked so sad and tired. I remember repeating this word over and over again in my mind so I wouldn't forget it: Auras, auras, auras.

I also made a promise to myself to be better, to help my mum more, and to make sure I earned a lot of money so she wouldn't have to work so hard to keep the roof over *my* head. It was my fault that my mum was so tired, and that's why she didn't like me; I had to make it right, or that's what I believed.

When we arrived home, I made her a cup of tea and went upstairs to my bedroom, opened my encyclopedia on the human body and looked for the word auras in the index. Nothing on auras. Nothing at all. Back then, we didn't have the internet, and I don't just mean my family didn't have internet, but no one had internet. It wasn't a thing. I'm of the generation where TV remote controls were not a thing. I wanted to visit the local library to learn about auras, but I wasn't allowed to go by myself. When I went to school, I looked in the library books and found nothing. What were they? What did they mean? I wanted to know.

I paid extra attention in science classes, but the knowledge in my geography, science and humanities soon distracted me because I was fascinated with the world. I would be in natural science with Mrs Richards after chemistry lessons with Mr. Baddeley, and the dots just kept connecting for me. I could see how we were so connected to everything and everyone. Then I started to see possibilities: *"If this is connected to that, and that is connected to this, then surely this is possible, and anything is possible!"* Thoughts going through my mind before the words, "Dawn Bates, STOP daydreaming!"

The thing was, I wasn't daydreaming. I was creating! Creating connections right there in class, and the possibilities for myself were becoming endless. "Just imagine...." was how so many of my internal thoughts began.

Being told off by the teachers for daydreaming became a daily occurrence. I would get excited about some of the things I was thinking and share them with classmates who made fun of me. I would go home and be excited to share my lessons and ideas, only to be shut down by my mum because there was work to be done, and told, "You live in a fantasy land, you do, young lady".

After a while, I knew my ideas and images had to be kept a secret. I couldn't share them with anyone. No, they were my secrets because just like the auras, the silver raindrops, feeling the earth spinning, and the images in the clouds. If people knew, they would only think me crazy. I knew the more I shared with my mum, the more she would repeat 'there you go again, thinking you're better than the rest of us', 'We're just not good enough for you, are we?', 'you and your bloody books, daydreams and fantasies' and accusing me of 'getting ideas above my station'.

I realised that even though Mum had bought me the books, she was too busy or too tired to listen to my 'ramblings' and ideas. My dad[1] would often raise an eyebrow, answering, "I dunno" if I shared an idea or asked a question, especially if he was busy in the garden or asleep in *his* chair,

---

[1] My dad is my stepdad, not my father. He has been my dad since the day he came into my life; and as the saying goes, "any male can be a father, but it takes a special kind of man to be a dad"

because he was also too tired from work. And I say *his* chair because it was. No one else was allowed to sit in it. Only I was brave enough to sit in it. My brother, who is eighteen months older than I, tried it once. He got smacked around the side of the head, so he never sat in the chair again. I would get lifted out of the chair by the top of my arms and booted up the backside. It would hurt, especially as my dad had a firm grip and used to be a footballer. For some reason, I thought this was some kind of game that Dad and I played. I wasn't being smacked around the head, for one thing, just kicked up the bottom.

Most nights after school, I'd be in my bedroom alone reading. I would read novels, my book of Psalms, dictionaries, and encyclopedias on every subject I could imagine. I'd read them, then re-read them, and when I learnt something new at school, I'd dive into the books in the library. And if I weren't reading, I'd be playing my music and dancing around my bedroom, singing into a hairbrush. I was Madonna, Diana Ross, Tiffany, or Tina Turner, and I would sing and dance until the moment I was told to "shut that bloody racket up and stop jumping around up there!" by either one of my parents. If it wasn't raining, I'd put my cassette tapes into my Walkman and go and dance around and sing in the garden, until I was told to stop disturbing the neighbours or giving my mum a headache. I'd sing in the car until I was shouted at for making an awful, bloody noise, and then I'd get my books out and read or complete puzzles, challenging myself to finish a wordsearch before we arrived. I'd keep a tally of how many I could do in a certain time frame. I just wanted to make my mum and dad proud of me. I had to prove to them that I was good and that all their hard work was being rewarded.

The more I read, the more my insatiable thirst for knowledge grew. My curiosity about the world we live in was palpable. The more words I'd learn and find in the word searches, the more I would use them in conversation or my visions. The images in my mind were on a constant evolving loop, and I didn't want the movie in my mind to run out like the VHS tapes dad would use to record his and mum's programmes. I'd lock all these images and visions quietly away in the attic of my mind, ready for me to unlock them at night when everyone else was asleep. They kept me interested in lessons at school, and diary after diary would be filled with ideas on where I would travel, who I wanted to be, and how I wanted to live my life. The more I learnt, the more I added to my collection, the more excited I became, and yet, the more alone I felt.

No one I knew at home or school understood me. They didn't want to learn, didn't want to go off to the faraway lands because of the *bloody foreigners*. They didn't want to learn the languages of the students who came to the international farm camp in the village, but I did. Making up languages, I taught my sister some of the words. Languages were fun, and I loved talking with people. I wanted to talk about everything, and the more questions I asked the teachers, the more I got bullied. With my head being smashed against brick walls at school, constant teasing and taunting, being pushed in the corridors, and being made fun of in lessons, the more my mother's haunting words about not being likeable were confirmed. I made friends, but didn't believe they liked me. I grew up not trusting people, not feeling safe and not feeling wanted.

My grandparents lived a ten-minute bike ride away or a twenty-minute walk through the fields, and grandad would teach me about gardening while my nanny taught me about baking. I was more interested in eating the baked goods than following the rules of baking. There was no freedom to create in baking. It was all so precise - except when we got to decorate. Life with my grandparents was peaceful. Grandad was always singing and dancing the 'aye aye ippy ippy aye aye' and Nanny would be singing her church hymns. Home was unsettling because of the arguments. I can't remember much about them, but they always included my dad smacking either me or my brother. My younger sister was hardly ever in trouble, leaving my brother and me to wonder if she was our half-sister. My mum and father[2] split up before my brother had even started school, and there are only four and a half years between my brother and sister, with me, the fat little piggy in the middle, who loved her books.

Discovering alcohol in my early teens and drugs around the age of fifteen was the escape I needed from the arguments and loneliness at home. Puberty hit hard, and the 'puppy fat' started to fall away due to long bike rides with my nanny, and being selected for the netball, rounders, and hockey teams at school. I made new friends, but again, my mum's words came dancing around in the back of my mind, *"The girls on the team are only being nice to me so we win matches."* The more others said they liked me, the more I distrusted them. How could they like me if my mother didn't? Surely that wasn't a possibility.

## Raving

At the age of fourteen, I got a job in the local fish and chip shop and a local restaurant. By the time I was sixteen, I was the restaurant manager of a high-end seventy-five-seater bistro, and I hired my mum to work as bar manager. By the age of eighteen, I became the assistant hotel manager of a two-hundred-bedroom hotel with a huge ballroom, two conference rooms, two restaurants and an orangery. I was making my own money. This allowed me the freedom to go out and pay for my books and clothes.

I discovered raving when a lad at school put on a 'rave room' during a school disco. Walking into the rave room to see what it was all about led me to discover a kind of music that would transform my life forever.

The energy my mum was repeatedly told I had would make me billions now had an outlet. The dancefloor became my friend, a place where I

---

[2] Father is the man who donated his sperm for me to come into existence. A man who told my mum to have me adopted because he didn't wish to contribute to my life, or my siblings.

could close my eyes and lose myself - or rather find myself. Feeling the rhythm and vibrations of the hard, fat bass lines and the acid rifts and techno beats of the music, I was transported to a whole other level of existence. Everyone and everything around me disappeared, and I had found a frequency like I had never known before.

For years, I'd read and heard about *'these ravers'* who destroyed farmlands, took copious amounts of drugs, and were a blight on society, and yet, I never saw anyone destroying farmlands or being a blight on society; quite the opposite. I was told I was an "inspiring individual and destined for greatness", with one customer telling me, "I wish my daughter were more like you; instead, she goes out raving every weekend, taking drugs and doing God knows what". If only he knew, and if only I knew how this was just another piece of an ever-increasing layering of myself that I hid from others.

My life became so compartmentalised and I became fractured, never able to be my whole self, due to my belief that if people knew the 'real me', then they'd never like me. Work colleagues remained colleagues at work. Yes, we would go out together after the shifts in hotels were over, but we were work colleagues who let our hair down together.

Raving friends were the friends I chilled out with after the madness of the dancefloor. They didn't know the side of me that was the geek, loved reading and learning, the woman who yearned to have her own business or who saw magic everywhere she looked.

And they certainly didn't know of the soul that was searching to make sense of the universal energy and blueprints of life.

The only person who saw and knew all of me was ramO. The man they called the 'Techno Terrorist' because he loved his techno almost as much as I did, and he wore a balaclava with his black combat trousers. The fact that he was also an Arab played a part in the name and appealed to the satirical and tongue-in-cheek humour that we both shared.

## Unraveling

ramO saw who I was, and with him, I felt safe to unravel. We would partake in mental gymnastics both with and without drugs. He'd regularly play devil's advocate as well as fiercely agree with me. I believed and trusted he had my back. We moved in together after two months, and after eighteen months, we bought our first home together. Shortly after we moved into our new home, we were engaged to be married.

Eighteen months after getting engaged, we were married, and I thrived. I had the safe space to be all of who I was with the one person I allowed to see all of me, and who encouraged me to show up in all areas of my life as ME. After nine months of being married, I was made redundant and took the opportunity to build my first business, whilst he went to work on clients' sites overseas.

Four years of living in Oxford, ramO and I moved north to Sheffield to live in what I was led to believe was the family home. From the very first day we arrived, I set up our new office and hit the ground running. I'd lined up meetings, joined a gym and started the house renovations. A week later, ramO and I went on holiday with my parents to the Greek island of Zante - a chance for us to build bridges and create a deeper family bond, as children were next on the horizon. A holiday was also desperately needed, so plenty of fun activities were booked as well as some downtime on the beach.

Thirty-six hours into the holiday, ramO suffered several grand mal seizures that lasted for at least thirty minutes each. Alone by myself at ramO's bedside in the small island hospital, my parents went off to enjoy the island together. It was confirmed that brain scans and surgery were needed, so with ramO heavily medicated by the hospital, we were flown home and escorted to the Royal Hallamshire Hospital in Sheffield by ambulance.

I continued the house renovations and building our business, and visited ramO in the hospital two to three times a day. I attended doctors' appointments and looked forward to the arrival of his dad from Oman. Baaba[3] and I had a great relationship. He'd been a doctor in Sheffield years before, so he knew many of the doctors in the hospital where ramO was being treated. My downtime was learning DIY, going to the gym, and learning more about how to run a business. I needed the business to work, I needed it to thrive, because it was the vehicle that would allow me to be a full-time mum to the boys I intended to have. ramO had to get better because I didn't want to be a single mum. Our home also had to be finished and ready for when the boys arrived, even though I was not yet pregnant.

Knowing what I wanted in the home, I'd already created a spreadsheet to determine how much investment was required. To create this income, I had to get smart with my business marketing, so I started my second business: expanding a business networking group I'd been a member of whilst living in Oxford. Setting up and launching both businesses, taking care of ramO, and continuing with the house renovations, I needed to attend the gym for my sanity every day.

Two years after his first seizure in Greece, ramO had the Gamma Knife surgery[4]. He was one of the very first patients to have it in the country. A couple of months later, when the doctors gave him the 'all clear to fly', we headed to Melbourne, Australia, for a holiday. Two weeks later, before we left Melbourne, we went for a walk on the beach, and I set the intention that our firstborn son would soon be conceived; and of course, just three months later, I was pregnant. The pregnancy was

---

[3] Baaba means dad in Arabic, and is also used as a term of endearment from a parent to a son, normally by the father to his son.
[4] https://www.gammaknife.org.uk/treatment/what-is-a-gamma-knife

blissful. The home was completed, businesses were going well, ramO was healing and back to work, and Khaalid was born just two months after my twenty-fifth birthday. We joked that he was more English than Arabic because he was born on the due date, bright and early. No delays or 'bada bukra'[5] with this son!

Our second son, Naasir, was born just four years later, both before the age of thirty, exactly as I had planned it; well, apart from me suffering from something called HELLP Syndrome[6] and doing motherhood alone due to ramO now working overseas on another client site. Business was good and kept me busy, as did developing community projects and taking care of the boys and the family home. I had no time to question whether ramO was being unfaithful or not, something others would ask me if I was worried about. Why would I be worried? We'd call each other several times a day and be on the phone working in silence with the occasional comments, ideas shared, and conversations.

With board positions within the Chambers of Commerce and Regional Regeneration Committees, I was harnessing the power of my energy, my inner geek and insatiable desire for knowledge, and being a worthy human being.

Everything in life was coming together:
First home before I was twenty-one - check!
Married before twenty-one - check!
My own business - check!
Two boys, four years apart - check!
Spiritual journey underway - check!

Life was great. Busy, but great. The boys attended meetings and events with me, and I was not just a full-time businesswoman succeeding in

---

[5] Bada bukra literally means after tomorrow, a phrase many Arabs use to excuse delays or loosely plan for things without effort or a strong desire.
[6] https://www.preeclampsia.org/hellp-syndrome

everything I set my mind to; I was also a full-time mum who took care of my fitness, strength, and energy. I felt like the luckiest woman alive, except for the fact that my parental family was almost a distant memory.

Creating my own family, I was able to understand what it meant to love another human, and whilst this was an incredible, all-consuming experience of joy (and tiredness!), my relationship with my parents and siblings began to deteriorate even further. Distance was growing because I'd married a *'bloody foreigner'*; one who was so intelligent my parents couldn't relate to him, or rather *didn't want to* relate to him. My parents are a product of their upbringing, generation and access to education, and the local area, which they never ventured away from.

My life and who I was becoming, or rather revealing who I truly was to the world, confronted my parents on many levels; and if they didn't like me before I showed them all of who I was, they certainly didn't like me now.

Or did they?
Honestly, I had no idea.

I thought I did, but with every twist and turn of my life's journey, the more I travelled, the more I succeeded, the less my parents *appeared* to want to know me. Through my critical illness, my parents never showed up for me, and just three years after our youngest son was born, ramO and I moved to Egypt to become closer to his family[7]. We didn't move because my family were not interested; we genuinely moved because we wanted our sons to have a relationship with their cousins, aunties, and uncles - and, of course, their grandparents.

---

[7] To learn more about the event sup until this point in my life, please visit https://dawnbates.com/fridaybridge

# Expat Life

Living in Egypt allowed us to get to know both sides of ramO's family as we travelled regularly to Lebanon, where Baaba's side of the family, the Palestinian side of the family, lived. Baaba and I loved the quiet rural life, books, cooking and enjoyed mystical discussions. His mother was the polar opposite, and yet, we were very similar in a lot of ways: Strong. Outspoken. Highly intelligent, and we loved our sons fiercely. The love she had for her firstborn son, Omar aka ramO, would cause an irreparable rift that would last until she took her final breath.

Life in Egypt was everything I expected it to be and more. With the Arab Spring unfolding and living through the Egyptian Uprising, things were tense. ramO and I had our ups and downs, and I became a teacher, a childhood dream I'd forsaken due to a lack of finances my parents had for a university degree in teaching. In Egypt, I was free to teach the way I believed would be the best way, even if it caused me a plethora of problems with the faculty staff.[8] My teaching style gifted my students a deep understanding of how to decode content and generate their own understandings, knowing there were no right or wrong answers when it came to reading comprehension. Each of their viewpoints was valid based on who they were, their life experiences and understanding of the words. Rote learning was not something I encouraged. They had a brain, they had feelings, and they had ideas; all that was needed was a cauldron to mix them all, create magic within themselves and unleash their fullest potential out into the world so they could thrive.

I loved teaching. Seeing the eyes of my students light up and their faces fill with smiles when they figured something out or achieved something

---

[8] To discover more about my life in Egypt, please visit https://dawnbates.com/walaahi to purchase my second book about life and times in Egypt during the Egyptian Uprising.

others had told them they couldn't was a wonderful gift; yet, this gift took away a lot of time with my boys. I fell asleep at the dinner table after a day in the classroom. At night, I'd be marking and making resources. I had no work-life balance because I was the main income earner. The money from the family home we were letting back in England never seemed to cover very much, and it was only when we returned to England years later that I discovered why.

Egypt offered me the anonymity I needed to figure out who I was, what I wanted and revisit parts of myself that had become a happening rather than a choice. Far too many times in life, we find ourselves just caught up in the rolling hours, the discovery of new choices, and the awe those choices have on others, that we forget about our own why for making those choices.

Hanging the paintings and worksheets up for my class children, painting the murals for them to learn from, reminded me of why I wanted to become a mum in the first place, and why I loved teaching. It was also a great time for me to simplify my thinking and step back from being in my life to observing it from the outside.

Was this the life I wanted?
Was I being the woman I truly knew myself to BE?
Was this life allowing me to become the mother, the human, and the woman I wanted to become?

The woman buried deep inside of me kept whispering in my ear, kept nudging me away from the classroom, telling me to breathe, to uncover the woman I was destined to become.

I knew I had to leave the school, and the moment I chose to leave, events unfolded which allowed this to happen. I clashed with many of the women in the school because I would not conform to the corruption and bitchiness that unfolded every day. I was told I was 'more Arab' than the Egyptian teachers because they were so desperate to become Westernised. Then there was the resentment that my Egyptian husband had chosen an English wife instead of an Egyptian wife. Plus, I could return to Britain - or go to any part of the world I wanted without trouble. There was a lot stacked against me, but I had grown up not being liked and believing I wasn't likeable, so it was just time to choose me and do what my soul kept nudging me to do - serve the children to the best of my ability and create another layer of freedom in my life. I created resources for my children in the classroom, gave them out, and the next day, I left, leading my boys out of the school into a taxi and went home.

Our unschooling days had begun, and we enjoyed the freedom it gave us immensely. The boys led with the subjects; I backed it up with the curriculum essentials. We laughed, we relaxed, we had fun, and every day we had a new classroom. This level of freedom was bliss-FULL, and the boys and I became closer with each new day. Our home library grew, and the boys could choose any book that interested them, rather than one that matched twenty other students. This autonomy, the agency of self, leaving the school had given us was the release of another deep breath I didn't know I was holding in. The boys and I would have lessons on the faluka[9], taking a picnic for lunch and dinner, books, crayons, and just spending the day sailing up and down the Nile and floating in the little inlets along the way.

Our knowledge of global politics deepened as I taught the boys Egyptian and Arabic history to help explain what was going on with the Uprising that was unfolding. They learnt about human rights and social justice, and how we need to fight for the freedom of others as we would our freedom, because if the human rights of others are not recognised, then neither are ours. No one is free until we're all free. This led to philosophical debates and a realisation that I was still not free to

---

[9] Faluka is the Arabic word for a sailboat

be me. My mother's words still haunted me, and parts of me were still hidden.

The boys and I spent a lot of time together on our own when living in Egypt, as ramO was working with the BBC to cover various stories across Egypt. I'd pretty much raised the boys alone when we were in Britain, and now, for different reasons, I was raising them alone again. Even when ramO was home, he wasn't present. He was working on various projects, and I would soon know what kind of projects they were.

## Back To Britain

We'd originally planned to stay in Egypt for at least five years, but once Sisi was elected president and Mohammed Morsi was imprisoned following the military coup, that was it.[10] I enrolled the boys back into the private boys' school that they had attended before we'd left to live in Egypt. The boys and I were excited to move back into the family home, that was until ramO told me his mum was selling it; a choice that would leave me and my boys homeless. With relations so bad with my mum and dad, the only option available to us was my father's home, four hours away from Sheffield, where the boys would attend school. The boys slept on blankets on the sparse bedroom floor, and I slept in an armchair for the entire time we were there.

I'd often be wondering about how - and why - this was all happening. I couldn't believe my mother-in-law was selling the family home, and that we wouldn't get any money from the sale of it. Having invested close to £100,000 in renovating it since living there. I was furious. ramO was quiet on the whole situation and did nothing to defend the boys and me from his mother's actions. I was not impressed in the slightest. Why was he being such a coward and not providing for us?

---

[10] You can read more about my life in Egypt and the Egyptian Uprising in my second book Walaahi https://dawnbates.com/walaahi

A month after returning to Britain, ramO called to let me know Baaba had died in a freak rainstorm whilst driving home from his shift at the hospital as a Cardiologist. My world collapsed around me. I wailed from a part of me that I didn't know existed and slid down the cupboard doors in the kitchen. Losing Baaba on top of my mother-in-law making us homeless was a whole other level of confusion. Had the world fallen off its axis, I don't think it would have impacted me more. Baaba was the dad I'd always wanted; supportive, encouraging, helpful, engaged, and playful with the boys. He was the perfect role model for the boys, and now he was gone. ramO was due back from Egypt in just a few weeks, so I had to keep my head together, push down the grief and get on with finding a home for me and the boys in Sheffield.

In all of this chaos and the events of the previous decade, I had pretty much lost sight of who I was and how everything was connected. I had forgotten all about auras, declaring what I wanted for it to happen, and hadn't journaled or kept a gratitude journal for quite some time. It was time to start it again, and no sooner than I begun imagining our new home, an estate agent from Sheffield called to let me know he had a property that had come on the market that was a little dated and needed updating, but when he sent me the details, it was just where I imaged it to be, and had all the features I was looking for. It seemed my magic was back.

It took me less than two weeks to organise the move. I felt excited, empowered, and ready to start this new chapter in our lives. The thing was, the Universe had even more in store for me than I could ever imagine, and would soon deliver, transforming our lives forever in the most unimaginable way possible.

Whilst I'd been in Egypt, I had written my first book, and I had an email from my publisher telling me it was to be showcased at the London Book Fair. Talk about excited! And yep, that was another 'tick!' on the checklist of life. I had two months to prepare and organise things for my week away in London, and for ramO to return to live with us in England on the Sunday after the London Book Fair. It was going to be a busy weekend, but one that the boys and I were so looking forward to. Our family was going to be back together again for this new chapter.

When the boys and I arrived at Heathrow to collect ramO, he was distant. Back in Sheffield with the boys setting up the board game 'Mouse Trap' at the dining room table, ramO dropped the bombshell I never saw coming. "I want a divorce." The world slowed down. There was to be no negotiations, no working it out, and all because he'd been cheating on me the whole time we'd been together, something I later bluffed out of him. It was the ultimate betrayal. The only one I had ever trusted enough to be all of who I am. It turned out he hadn't ratified our marriage certificates from Egypt, so we were not even legally married. It made divorce quick, easy, and cheap. I changed my name by deed poll to Ms Dawn Bates instead of Mrs Dawn Bates and walked away, telling him the boys would be his judge, not some stranger in a courtroom. He was free to see the boys whenever he wanted and pay whatever he wanted towards their future.

My mother's words came back with furious vengeance. Had I just been his access to a British passport? Or just a womb in which to conceive and grow his children, ensuring his family line continued? To this day, after everything I have learnt about him, I doubt he ever loved me, but none of this matters anymore because I have the most incredible young men as my sons, young men I'm truly honoured and privileged to be the mother of.

Ten days after ramO dropped the bombshell, he moved to the US to be with his fiancée, something he announced on Facebook before we'd even managed to tell any of our friends. Not only was I deeply hurt by this, but I couldn't believe he'd been so thoughtless and tacky. Then I checked myself and realised his infidelity had been both, so why was I surprised?

I had a lot of unpacking to do, not just in the house, but of my emotions, thoughts and all the hopes and dreams I had for me and the boys. I knew I had everything within me to provide for the boys and me, even if ramO didn't. I got to work, started studying, building my business, and sorting out all the household bills - something ramO had been responsible for paying. It was confronting how much was being paid out, but I kept on keeping on. That summer, the boys and I took a seven-week road trip around Britain. I took my laptop because I was now making a profit and wanted to keep the momentum going. During the road trip, I was preparing the boys for their Duke of Edinburgh Awards[11] and ended up starting a new relationship with an old friend. Things were looking up... and then events took an unbelievable turn for the worse. I was arrested, put in a police cell for fifty-seven-and-a-half hours, and I was made to sign the boys over to social services, who placed them into foster care.

Upon my release from the dingy jail cells, the boys were returned to me, and now the fight was on to clear my name. I worked harder than I'd ever worked before. No one messes with my boys and gets away with it. No one. What the police had done, and the justice system allowed to happen, let's say I found my fire. ALL OF IT! The Celtic fire, the Mama fire, the Sagittarian fire, and the Feminine Fire all unleashed.

The boys and I made the best of everything. They changed schools, I went without food to feed them, and worked my arse off to build my current business. I was exhausted from studying the various aspects of law needed to win the case. I found case precedents, worked long hours, *and* wrote my second book, *Walaahi*[12] - a first-hand account of living

---

[11] https://www.dofe.org/
[12] You can purchase a copy of my second book, all about our life living in Egypt through the Uprising by clicking on this link https://dawnbates.com/walaahi

through the Egyptian Uprising, which went on to become an International Bestseller on three continents in just seven days. I was determined our lives would not be severely impacted, so we'd have picnics in the park, BBQs at every opportunity, and we still had our weekend road trips.

Preparing the case myself, with the support of a lawyer who guided me, I refused a bribe from the prosecutor fiscal, stating, "I'd rather go to jail for telling the truth than lie and give truth to their lies". My solicitor advised me otherwise, but there was no way I was going to have a conviction for something I had not done. I went on to win the case. I may have had debts totalling half the mortgage of my first home in Oxford, but there was no way I was going to go to prison due to the corruption, sexism and racism of Police Scotland officers and the Scottish Judicial system.

Things really couldn't have gotten any worse-until they did. And it is this last event that led me to be on the yacht in Vanuatu, crying my eyes out. I'd ended the relationship with my then-partner, and then met him for a drink a week later to smooth things over. I remember all the events of that evening up to the point of waiting for the bus to take me home to my boys. Except I didn't make it home. I woke up the next morning, no clothes on my bottom half, in a lot of pain and heavily drugged. I had no idea where I was, and lying next to me was a man I'd never met and would never speak with.

The boys were at school when I returned home, and I was so out of it that the only person I knew to reach out to was my ex-husband, who'd returned to Britain nine months after he had left to be with his now ex-fiancé. He came straight away to help me. He helped me figure a few things out, contacted the man I'd just finished with and encouraged me to attend the local rape crisis centre. They examined me, took my statement and then the necessary forensic evidence and said they would inform the police, keeping the evidence on file in case the man could be identified. They said it was unlikely anything would happen as I was so heavily drugged; it would be his word against mine. Needless to say, I didn't hear from the police.

## Choosing Me

I knew I was not in any fit state to parent my boys because I was in no fit state to take care of myself. Pushing down the pain, taking the medication, including anti-HIV tablets every day for a month, I also buried the trauma, putting on a brave face for my boys, and I honoured my promise to them of a trip to New Zealand to see family and friends. The Universe may have sent curveballs my way, but there were so many other blessings, such as a beautiful Cavapoo pup, who we named Chewy. She mated with Kelt, my shadow and a Lhasa Apso dog the boys and I had rescued from a pet shop in Egypt, who'd become part of our family. Selling the pups financed our New Zealand adventure, so I knew I still had my manifesting magic. I just had to figure out why there was a shit storm of trauma circling my energetic field.

And so, when the boys flew home from New Zealand after a five-week holiday, I stayed to sort my head out and do some deep healing.

How had my dream life and all my plans gone so badly wrong?
Why was I attracting such trauma in my life?
What lessons did I have to learn?
Who, other than myself, had to learn from these events in my life?
What needed to happen for me to release myself from this generational cycle of abuse?

I went deep. Dark nights of the soul were commonplace, as were the flashbacks, nightmares, and days of staying in bed not wanting to face the world. Suicidal thoughts danced in my mind almost daily, but I knew I couldn't leave my boys without their mother. I needed them, and they needed me. So, I dug deep into every area of my life, my ego, and my identity.

Energy healing, past life regressions, cord cuttings, journalling, you name it, I did it. And slowly but surely, I came back to myself. I got out of bed every day. I danced, I ran, I lifted weights, I sang, and I sailed the world.

My boys cheered me on every step of the way, and we set plans for them to join me in the different countries I visited. I researched material for my books and chose to turn my research into a body of work for my PhD. I wrote book after book after book. I started coaching and publishing other people's books, built a six-figure business, avoided lockdown during Covid due to the various locations I was in, and flew my boys out to be with me in multiple countries.

I found my way back to myself by choosing me, by choosing to heal myself from the pain and trauma and generational patterns that have plagued the women in my family for generations. I chose and declared that the trauma stopped with me.

And it has.

I knew I didn't want girls; I just didn't know the reason.
My sons are now grown adults, and they are protectors, not predators, violators, or abusers.

Arriving back in Britain (again) after all the healing I'd done, I unravelled. I needed to because it allowed me to take the only course of proper action: to take the system to court for gross negligence and systemic failure.

I won the case.
For me,
For others,

But sadly, even though the police were able to identify the man who violently raped me, due to a previous crime and a semen sample he'd been requested to give before, he still walks free, as he would in many countries around the world.

So I am not done.
There is another book to write.
And this time, I am wiser, stronger, and more learned.

I learned the system isn't broken; it is working exactly how the powers that be want it to.
All we have to do, ladies, is own our ovaries on a whole new level, fuelling the fires of men and women around the world to create powerfully positive social change.

And so it is done.

# Reflections

# Reflections

## Heatherjane Dangerfield
## Wales

Heatherjane Dangerfield wondered what she wanted to be when she grew up, and in her forties, she found her dream job working with volunteers in a Charity that helped bereaved parents such as herself.

Passionate about helping others and making a difference, Heatherjane is a beacon of hope and joy, tenderness, and empathy in all the right measures, which makes sure those she works with - as colleagues and clients - are always taken care of in the way that supports them best.

Her son Xander never lived, but through her, she is making sure he is always remembered, and his legacy lives on.

An only child and divorced, Heatherjane is surrounded by loving and supportive family and friends who have encouraged her to follow her dreams.

She is the fur-baby Mama to her rescue dog Jax, who, in his way, has rescued her.

Heatherjane currently volunteers for various charities and has been supporting families and health professionals for over eighteen years.

# Are You Better Yet?

Dave and I met in 1996 whilst I still lived with my parents, in my childhood bedroom. After three years of resisting him, I agreed to go on a date with him. We talked so much about the future and how much we both wanted children that a week later, we were engaged. Two years later, we had the perfect church wedding. We finally moved into our own home in January 2002, and I was an emotional mess due to the stress of house-hunting, my great uncle's passing away, and lots of changes at work. I had a breakdown and was given antidepressants. Everyone around me was shocked as they'd only seen the upbeat me, a mask I wore so people wouldn't see the real me.

My thirtieth birthday arrived, and the ticking clock was getting louder. It was time to start trying for a baby, which was put on hold in October 2002 due to a car crash, which put my spine out of alignment. In January 2004, I became very broody as family members were pregnant and I was seeing new babies and cute outfits everywhere.

Then in early February, I booked a trip to Prague. On the way to the Passport Office to renew my passport, I realised my period was late. The next day, I bought three pregnancy tests. I told myself I was only going to check so that I knew what to pack for our trip, but in my heart, I so wanted this to be it. The second I got home, I ran upstairs to the bathroom. I ruined the first two tests, and when the third test said "PREGNANT", it was mind-blowing. I don't think I've ever been through so many emotions, " Will I be a good mum?", "Can I cope with the pain of childbirth?" "Am I ready for this?", "I'm having a baby!". I was scared, overjoyed, sobbing, and so emotional all in a few minutes. I rang Dave and had to leave a message. It felt like a lifetime waiting for him to ring back. He was overjoyed and started talking to my stomach, and I became obsessed with cheese and pickle rolls[13] and I didn't even like pickles!

During our trip to Prague, we stood on the Charles Bridge discussing Vin Diesel filming XXX in the same location. We thought Xander would be a cool name for a boy. I was so emotional and tired that we returned home a day early. When we got back, we invited our parents over for food and gave them a little bag with booties in it. The joy and excitement from them was overwhelming and lovely.

At six weeks, I experienced spotting, which was scary. My boss rang Dave, and we went to the Early Pregnancy Assessment Unit (EPAU) and saw our baby's heartbeat for the first time. Thankfully, everything was okay. We had another scan at eight weeks, and gave the baby the nickname of 'Peanut'.

On Dave's birthday in April, I woke to a bed full of blood. When you're half asleep and realise the bed is wet, then realise it is blood, it is a horrendous and scary moment. I remember frantically brushing my teeth whilst Dave was ringing my parents for a lift and thinking, "I refuse to lose this baby on his birthday." My parents took us directly to A&E. I was eleven weeks and six days pregnant.

The A&E staff were lovely and made sure I was comfortable. Although I had no pain, I was losing clots of blood. My heart was breaking at the thought of losing our baby. Dave and I talked about what we'd do if we lost Peanut, but tried to look forward into the future. We later learned that my cervix seemed closed, and I wasn't losing the baby. They couldn't scan until the following day, so I went home and rested. The next twenty-four hours were the longest of our lives to date, and not the best birthday for Dave.

---

[13] Rolls are the British word for bread rolls, also known as breadcakes in Sheffield, baps in the Midlands and many other places, cobs in Leicestershire, and barms in Merseyside. Welcome to British English!

The following day, we were a bag of nerves and emotion. Seeing Peanut on the scan looking so calm and relaxed as if to say, "hey mum, what's the problem!?" was emotional. To date, it is still my favourite scan photo. I was exactly twelve weeks. I asked the Registrar where all the blood and clots had come from, and he just kept telling me, "The baby's okay". Thankfully, my GP explained what may have happened, and confirmed my Rhesus negative blood group was rare; something the A&E were concerned about.

Eight weeks passed with no issues, and finally, my twenty-week scan date arrived. Lots of people told me I was having a boy, but I was determined they were wrong. I wanted a little girl, so when the scan showed a boy, I felt robbed. I was so upset, my little girl, who I'd named Amy May, had been taken from me and replaced with a boy. I feel so ashamed of how I felt that day. The baby was healthy, and I should've focused on that. I often felt that maybe I'd been punished due to my ungratefulness for being offered a healthy baby boy.

After the scan, we went shopping for some baby boy clothes, and the name that we'd chosen whilst standing on the Charles Bridge in Prague for a boy, finally had a place in my heart. Xander Dangerfield Coombs was alive and kicking.

My cousin Nicola also found out she was having a boy, and it looked to be exciting times ahead. Both daddies started to plan their sons' social lives: Boxing, swimming, rugby and football. These boys were not going to be able to sit still. Xander started kicking, and if someone wanted to feel him, I'd feel him turning away, as if to say, "Get off!" He always moved closer to the sound of Dave's voice, no matter how uncomfortable I was. Sometimes I'd start sobbing as I couldn't breathe properly until he moved. He was very stubborn. Just like his dad.

My energy levels increased, and I needed a glucose diabetes check due to my weight. Everything came back as normal, which was a surprise to my doctor, as she was quite adamant that *'bigger ladies had more problems'* and ordered another diabetes test and more scans. She spoke to me as though I were something she'd scraped off her shoe. I cried most of the way home. No one should be made to feel the way she made me feel that day. To make me feel better, Dave took me shopping and we bought Xander the Liverpool away kit, complete with little socks.

## 1st September 2004

With my hospital bag packed, the nursery ready, and clothes for Xander, I was ready to start maternity leave on the 3rd of September.

Nature had a different idea. At 4 am on 1st September, I awoke to more spotting. I was thirty-six weeks pregnant. Dave woke up, rang my parents, and off to the maternity ward we went. I didn't feel concerned; I knew if they delivered now, he'd be okay. As the midwife, doctor, registrar, Dave and the anaesthetist all took a look, I lay there thinking how I wish I'd taken the time to shave my legs! Both Xander and I were on monitors and doing okay. I was given some steroids and an anti-D injection due to my blood group, then more steroids twelve hours later to help build Xander's lungs up. I needed to be kept in for observation, so Dave and my parents were sent home.

The next day, I was bored. The bleeding had stopped, Xander felt fine, and I wanted to go home. After evening visiting time was over, I sat watching the news, and realised I needed the toilet. What I saw sitting on the toilet will stay with me forever. I was haemorrhaging. I pulled the emergency cord, and the midwives came, wheeled me into a side room, where a midwife and a student midwife were waiting. The midwife tried to find a heartbeat, but the silence in the room was deafening. I kept asking if Xander was okay. The student midwife came and held my hand. Finally, after what felt like forever, the midwife left the room to return with the registrar and the scanner. The image on the scanner wasn't what I was used to seeing. My active little boy was not moving. The registrar put down the Doppler and said the baby was dead, and walked out of the room just as Dave walked in. Dave didn't know whether to follow him for more information or come to me. I felt the student midwife tighten her grip on my hand, or maybe it was mine on hers, I don't know. What I do remember is hearing a primal scream like an animal in pain, and thinking how sad it sounded before I realised it was me making the noise. I remember repeating over and over, "Babies don't die in real life, only in soap operas. I am a real person, not an actress! My baby is alive!" I remember saying, "I can still feel him kicking," but the midwife explained it was mother nature kicking in and my labour was starting. I wanted them to get Xander out. He was dead, so why didn't they take him out? The midwife explained that a C-section was a big operation and that a lot of mums felt robbed when they had done this, so they were going to induce me instead and let nature take its course. I've experienced close losses in the past, but nothing can ever prepare you for the loss of a child. It is not the natural order of things. Our baby boy, Xander, was pronounced dead at 10.31 pm.

Dave had the unpleasant task of informing our families. The midwife offered me sleeping tablets, but I wanted to try and get my head around what was happening. My parents arrived and slept on the floor of the waiting room. Due to the blood I'd lost, I was on a drip. Every time I needed the toilet, Dave would carry my drip and come with me. We joked that he was my water boy. We spent a lot of time in the bathroom that evening, as it was so small, it felt safe. We planned Xander's funeral in those early hours, the songs, the vicar and what he was going to wear. I didn't want a hymn, but Dave wanted 'Morning Has Broken' as it was something Xander would have sung in school. We talked about how things like this could make or break a couple and how communication would be needed to get us through. We were so close that evening in our loss.

The following day, I was moved into a bigger room with a sofa, and the medical staff started the process of induction. News was starting to filter through to our friends, extended families and work colleagues; some rang and a few visited. They cried with us and also made us laugh in such a difficult time. Twenty-four hours later, I started to feel labour pains, but they were still weak after two attempts at inducing me. That night was the first showing of Doc Martin with Martin Clunes. I remember feeling I needed something to laugh at, and for an hour, it helped. Dave was lying on a sofa trying to get to sleep, and I was on the bed with my drip. We heard seven babies born that night. Hearing the mum's in labour pain and then their babies crying killed us, knowing our baby would be born without cries other than the ones we would give.

Amongst many of my questions, I wondered what I'd done wrong. Why was I being punished?

## Meeting Mummy's Boy

In the words of the famous "Papa Was A Rolling Stone" song, "It Was The 3rd September, A Day I Will Never Forget".

My labour pains finally started to increase, and the hospital asked the bereavement counsellor to speak with us about what would happen next. I was given pethidine, and finally, my waters broke. I couldn't seem to work out how to scream, push and breathe in the gas and air all at the same time, so I gave up on the gas and air. My midwife reminded me of my breathing exercises from antenatal; I replied, "They don't start until next Monday!". She explained that if I wanted to have limited stitches, then I had to listen and channel my 'lovely scream' into a push; so I pushed.

After a few hours in labour, Xander was born at 2.43 pm, weighing 5lb 5.5oz. My midwife quickly cleaned him up and dressed him. Cathy, my midwife, passed Xander to Mum whilst I delivered the very damaged and grey placenta. Xander was then handed to me, and I held the most precious gift I've ever been given. I'm so glad they didn't just "get him out" as I'd originally wanted, and so grateful that I'd had the privilege of experiencing childbirth and being pregnant.

Xander was perfect, so long and gorgeous. His hair was dark ginger with tight curls, and his fingers were long. I held him to me and told him how much he was loved and wanted, and how I would always keep his memory alive. I told him how sorry I was that he'd been taken from us before he'd gotten to know us, all whilst trying not to cry over him, as I wanted him to have a positive experience of his parents.

When they finally came in to do my stitches, they offered me gas and air, but I didn't feel I needed it as I'd just given birth to my boy without much pain relief. As the needle went in, I realised I did and took a breath of gas and then understood the joy of it! At one point, I think I was offering it around to everyone!

Dave's family arrived, and we let them have their time whilst we took the opportunity to take a shower. Tears were shared, photographs were taken, and memories were made. Dave and I had already discussed a post-mortem and wanted, no - needed to know - what had happened, so consent was given.

Dave was on a rollercoaster of emotions. He hadn't known if he wanted to be in the room when Xander was born. He was unsure whether he wanted to see or hold Xander. He decided not to hold him, and I knew he'd regret it. I pretended to slightly lose my hold on Xander, giving the impression he was slipping from me. I told Dave I was tired and needed to put Xander back in the cot. Dave took him from me and gave him a quick kiss before placing him in the cot. I told him later what I'd done, and he was grateful I had.

Thanks to my dad and others, we have photos of Xander, and Cathy also gave us a little booklet which had the prints in and details of his weight, etc, along with a couple of locks of his hair; one in the book and one in an envelope so I could place it in a locket. Protocols weren't shared, so we didn't know we could've had him blessed, and even though we're not religious, I would've liked to have done that. As Xander was going for a post-mortem, the hospital team couldn't guarantee what would happen with his clothes or his blanket. It was suggested we take those home with us, and he was put into a baby grow. Cathy asked if I wanted to leave the room first or if I wanted her to remove Xander from the room before we left. Such a simple question, but so difficult in reality to answer. I decided I wanted to leave him within the room, as if I was saying goodnight to him in his nursery. We kissed him goodbye and goodnight and headed home with empty arms and broken hearts. The six hours with him may seem like a long time, but no time would've been enough as we were meant to have him for our lifetime.

## Home

Leaving the hospital without Xander was one of the hardest things I've ever had to do. I'd left the house a few days earlier, so excited to be bringing him home to his nursery, his clothes, his toys. Instead, I came home broken and empty. The journey home was so strange, looking out of the window of the car and seeing people laughing and getting on with life. I felt as though I was on a merry-go-round that was going too fast, and everyone was starting to blur. How could they go about their day as if nothing had happened when my world had just been ripped apart and devastated in a way that could never be repaired?

Coming up the stairs and seeing the nursery in front of me broke me, and I quickly closed the door. Over the next few weeks and months, I would sit in the room and cuddle Xander's toys. I'd look in his wardrobe at the clothes. I wrote to him in his room, placing the letters in a silver Winnie the Pooh box that my mum and dad had had personalised for him.

The next day, my cousin came round with her new baby boy, Kaden. I held him close and told him about Xander. When he started to cry, I realised I'd never hear Xander cry and began crying, as did Nicola and Dave. When Nicola left, Dave asked her, "Bring Kaden again tomorrow?" We became Godparents to Kaden, and he is a huge part of our lives.

A health visitor arranged a visit, but I didn't know what a health visitor did. As far as I knew, they just weighed the baby. I asked if I had to see her, as I didn't want to speak to another health professional I'd never met. I was told I didn't. In some respects, I wish I had. I wish it had been explained how they could help and point me to what help was available. I felt very alone, but also didn't want to speak to people or anyone. Dave and I chose a special ringtone for those closest to us for when they rang.

Our family and friends were wonderfully supportive. We didn't want to face the world, and we didn't want to cook, so a bit of shopping or bringing food was wonderful to us. Sitting with us, buying us a memory box and an album so I could put some special bits in it were all very special. It was the practical help that helped us the most. I also didn't want to be alone in case the door or phone went, so when Dave did have to go out, the people who offered to sit with me were amazing and such a lifeline. Taking Dave to register Xander as stillborn, and sending flowers and cards. My Aunty Diane wrote a special poem for us, and I never read the cards until nine years later. I couldn't do it at the time. I should've been receiving congratulations cards, not sympathy cards. Work colleagues did a collection and named a star after Xander, and they also bought us a telescope so we could look at it properly. The star was in the Lion Cub constellation, as that's what he was, my little Simba.

Waiting to know when Xander would be released to us for the funeral felt like a lifetime. It didn't help matters that my milk arrived shortly after I arrived home from the hospital. Nature felt so cruel; giving a mother milk when she has no baby is a real kick in the teeth. Having to go to the mother and baby aisle in the supermarket to get nipple pads and maternity pads with other mums and their babies is so hard; so is going shopping for a new bra as your breasts get bigger and painful. Everywhere I turned, there were pregnant mums or new babies.

Whilst Googling one day, I found the charity SANDS (Stillbirth And Neonatal Death Charity)[14]. They shared advice on things to do for the funeral, such as writing a letter and placing it in the coffin. I'm so glad I found that site. I also looked at the support available, and although there was nothing in Cardiff, there were people they called 'befrienders', parents who'd experienced a loss themselves. I asked for the details of Pembroke, which was nearby.

The first email I wrote was probably the hardest. Being able to type and cry, releasing what I was feeling, was so freeing. When Donna, my befriender, replied, I started to realise I was not alone. Knowing what I was feeling was natural was such a relief. Some things I wrote, I didn't need a reply to; I just needed to get them out of my system. Donna was amazing. She really did save my life, reassuring me that it's natural when you've lost a baby to want to be a proper parent and be with your child. You go through such dark thoughts and emotions, and I think it was only the love for our parents that stopped us from doing something fatal. Donna showed me you can survive the devastation. I needed that and the hope that went with it.

Finally, a date for the funeral was given, and all the things we'd planned were starting to take shape. Dave and I both needed new clothes for the funeral as we wanted to make Xander proud. My mum and dad took us out for the day to get away from everything and clear our heads. A picnic in Brecon on a lovely day and a trip on the railway were

---

[14] https://www.sands.org.uk/

wonderful, although every time I caught myself smiling, I would feel so guilty. My son had died, how dare I be happy! There were quite a few tears that day, but getting out of the house was really what we needed. I just kept imagining Xander with us. I always like to believe he is with me, causing mischief wherever we go.

## The Funeral

Weeks earlier, I'd been planning a Christening, and now I was planning a funeral! Surely this is wrong; a child buries a parent, not a parent a child.

The vicar who'd married us a few years previously came out to talk to us about our wishes. Dave had practised saying, "More tea, vicar" all day, but when asked if he wanted a drink, the vicar politely declined. Poor Dave. There was so much to consider for the funeral. Which songs to have, what to dress Xander in, if we wanted the coffin at home before the service, if we wanted to go in front or behind the car carrying the coffin, who was to carry the coffin itself, which flowers to have; it was so overwhelming. To some, these might be simple questions, but I spent many hours thinking of the answers. In the end, the funeral directors made some of the decisions.

We chose to have a small service, with Dave reading the poem 'IF' as he had always promised himself he would one day read that to his son. He'd also carry the coffin and asked for 'Morning Has Broken' as the hymn. We both chose "Missing You" by Puff Daddy, and the Jim Davidson song, "Watching Over You" for the final curtain. The vicar was wonderfully supportive, even though I'm not religious and was feeling quite angry at this stage. I didn't understand how people could have lots of children roaming the streets in their nappies, not caring, and people like us who had wanted him so much had to say goodbye. I fell out with God at this point.

We'd picked out a little shirt, tie, waistcoat and trousers and a pair of dog slippers. In his coffin we placed a small rugby ball, his little donkey, a letter I wrote to him with messages to my nan's, a St Christopher that I'd had as a child for his safe journey to whatever the other side was, a lock of my hair and a photograph of the three of us.

The day of the funeral, I felt sick. I hadn't slept the night before and couldn't face food. I wanted this day to be erased. I shouldn't be having a funeral; Xander shouldn't be dead. The journey to the crematorium seemed such a long, quiet one. We were all lost in our thoughts. Getting out of the car and seeing his small coffin, I thought I was going to collapse. The vicar came to me and held my hand, but I wanted to hug my baby and for someone to make this nightmare go away. Instead of flowers, we asked for money to be donated to a local children's hospice in his memory. Dave was so brave carrying Xander's coffin and reading 'IF'. I was so proud of him. Seeing the curtains close was horrendous. I read afterwards that we could have requested them not to be closed, again something we hadn't been told.

One of the hardest things that day was looking over at my Bampy[15] Dangerfield and seeing him crying. I'd never seen him show emotion, and my son's dying had provoked that. The funeral may have triggered some memories as he and my nan had lost a few babies together, one of which was my uncle, who died at six months old due to pneumonia.

A death notice was placed in the local paper, and a reporter came out and talked to us about losing a baby. We told him how loved and wanted Xander was and how we'd heard so many babies born that night, how uncomfortable the room was for Dave and the general experience. We spoke about how we thought it was an uncommon experience, but found out there are nearly seventeen stillbirths a day.

Where to scatter Xander's ashes was something else we had to consider. We didn't want to bury them, but nowhere seemed quite right. My mum and dad suggested planting a tree in a pot and putting his ashes at the bottom, so the tree would grow and his ashes would be a part of it. We both loved the idea and asked if the tree could stay with them. I'm not green-fingered, and I was scared that he had died once in my care. I didn't want to kill him again.

Going to the crematorium and waiting in the office to collect our son was the oddest feeling. Coming home with a wooden box with his ashes instead of a car seat with a living baby in it is one of the most

---

[15] Bampy is a colloquial term for grandfather.

heartbreaking things ever. We held a little service in my parents' garden with family, and our nephew, who was six at the time, looked in the pot we were planting Xander in and had just placed the ashes and said, "I don't understand". I wish I could have explained it to him, but I didn't understand either. The box that held the ashes was lovely, even though his name was spelt wrong. A suggestion to turn the box into a jewellery box was a nice idea, so a new plaque was made, and the box was lined with fabric, ready for the letters I would write to Xander.

## Returning to work.

The weeks that followed the funeral were difficult. Dave returned to work and bought me a teddy bear, which we named Xander. When pressed, the bear would say "I love you", which both killed me but also helped me. A month to the day of giving birth to Xander, Dave and I became Godparents to Kaden. We were so honoured to be asked to be a big part of his life.

The midwife suggested I return to work after Christmas, but with the main focus being on Christmas and not me, I returned after a much-needed week away in Fuerteventura. I felt like a fraud being on maternity leave with no baby. It felt wrong. I wish I had listened to her.

Most people were wonderful, but some avoided me. Some people had not been told. I was asked questions such as "You're back early, how is the baby sleeping?" or "When are you bringing the baby in?". I'm not sure who felt more uncomfortable, them or me. I had a photograph of Xander that I insisted I put on my desk, and thankfully, no one challenged me.

Christmas Day, Dave and I kept busy; we had a house full for lunch and then a bigger house full for a buffet in the evening. Dave had been put on call and was under a lot of pressure to return to work. There were constant phone calls saying, "No pressure to come back, but the work on your desk is mounting". Even on the day of Xander's funeral, his boss rang to enquire if Dave was going on a training course. One of the most difficult things I found was when others brought their babies to work. I hadn't prepared myself for people to look at me with concern. I suffered from anxiety, felt the room was spinning, and as though I was going to pass out. My doctor asked how long I'd been having these attacks, and I said, "Since I'd had the baby. He then asked, "How old is the baby now?". The importance of reading patient notes.

On the morning of the post-mortem results, we approached the hospital desk of the antenatal department and saw pregnant women everywhere. My heart sank. I was so relieved when they took us to a small office and found somewhere to give us the results away from happy families. The consultant told us Xander was perfect. My placenta had abrupted, no rhyme or reason, it was "just one of those things", and there was a twenty-five per cent chance of it happening again in another pregnancy. He said that our registrar had rung him the morning of the 1st September to ask about doing a c-section, but as both Xander and I seemed okay, there was no reason for it. I guess we will never know if things would have been massively different had they done that c C-section. My placenta had grown an extra lobe, but I was told that wouldn't have made any difference, although it could explain the main bleeding I'd had early in my pregnancy. An agreement was made that in my next pregnancy, I would be closely monitored and given half an aspirin, which would help the baby stick better. I was also to be induced at thirty-eight weeks. I made a complaint about the registrar and his dealings with us, especially how he had informed us that the baby was dead. The consultant informed us that the registrar no longer worked at that hospital. Part of me felt happy about that and the fact that I would never see him again, but I felt unhappy that somewhere, he'd be dealing with another woman in the same way he dealt with me.

Mother's Day arrived, and Dave asked if I wanted a card and a present. I felt torn. People were telling me I was still a mum, but didn't a mum have children to show for it? I said no, then I said yes. Poor Dave must have been so confused about what to do for the best. In the end, both Dave and my parents bought me gifts as they couldn't bear the thought of me not having anything. It was such a difficult day, one I found harder as the years went on, knowing that he would have been making me cards in school.

## Sausage

At the end of April, just before another trip to Fuerteventura, I realised my period was late. I was so scared, and also excited. This time, I'd be closely monitored, and it would be different; I knew it would. I was a lunatic, though, constantly back and forth to the toilet, checking for bleeding. We told our immediate family, as we were so scared and really needed their support.

We weren't sure about going on holiday, but it had been booked a year before with my cousins, and Xander was on the booking. Ringing the travel agency to remove Xander and the baby cot from the booking was really difficult. Despite my reservations, the holiday went well and I got plenty of rest.

A six-week scan had been agreed, and it was such a relief to see the tiny bean and know I was pregnant. The excitement was short-lived lived though, as by the afternoon I'd started to spot. I'd hoped that it was due to the internal scan. I spoke to the Early Pregnancy Unit and was advised to have some bed rest. At eight weeks, we had another scan. We heard a strong heartbeat and saw our little sausage clear as a bell. We were over the moon and went to have some lunch and a nose around the baby shop. I started to feel really ill and had a cough, which was getting worse. The next day, I lay in bed coughing and felt something was wrong. I went to the toilet and I knew I'd passed my little Sausage. I was alone and bleeding heavily. I rang the EPAU, who told me to ring for an ambulance, leave the door open and sit close to the phone. I rang Dave, asked him not to contact anyone and told him I'd ring when I knew which hospital they were taking me to. It was all very surreal. I felt so calm and had stopped coughing. I felt I'd coughed my baby away.

There were no beds in either of the closest hospitals, so I was to be taken to one further away. I rang Dave as promised, and then realised the drip they'd put in me had blood in it and my jeans were soaked. I hadn't thought to bring spare trousers. With lights flashing and sirens going, I felt like I was watching from a distance. It didn't feel real.

I remember the nurse taking my details said to me, "You're only young, plenty of time to have more". I wanted to physically hurt her; she had no idea what I'd been through in the last eight months. I was moved to another area, and a lovely nurse arrived. She was my saving grace. She came with me when the porter took me down for a scan to confirm what I already knew. They placed me in a room full of pregnant women, happily waiting for their scans. I sat in a wheelchair, a blanket over me, as my jeans were in such a mess, and I just sobbed. Dave and my dad arrived while I was being checked in. Dave was holding my hand, and the nurse moved me to the corridor so I didn't have to sit with everyone else. The scan confirmed the baby was gone. Due to the heavy bleeding, the doctors wanted to monitor me for six hours, and then they'd move me to the gynaecology ward.

When I got to the ward, I was told I'd be kept overnight for observation. I didn't want that. I wanted to go home, but it was agreed that Dave could stay with me under the circumstances. The nurse came to take all my details, and I was so rude to her. She asked if I smoked. I answered that I was going to start smoking forty a day. She asked if I drank alcohol, and I said I was going to start drinking a litre a day. She asked my religion, and I asked her, "What God?!" As I say, I was not nice and I do regret that now. It wasn't her fault that I had lost another baby. Mum rang and shortly afterwards, the family started to arrive. Yet again, I felt I'd let them down.

I didn't sleep that night, and around mid-morning, after a shower and a visit from the doctor, I was discharged.

Yet another baby had left, and I now really needed that counselling as I was in fear of losing the plot. Losing Sausage had made me realise how much I was still grieving for Xander and how much I missed him. My Grampy had also passed away a few months after Xander, and now Sausage, all in eight months. I was so desperate to hold my baby.

Shortly after I'd returned to work, my dad was diagnosed with prostate cancer. I remember my manager hugging me and saying, "I'm not sure how much more you can take" I said, "Neither am I."

I would have terrible days when I wouldn't speak to anyone, not even Dave. Thankfully, work was amazing, and we devised a system where, on good days, I'd work a little extra, and it would then cover me for any bad days. Over the years, they became less, but for someone who doesn't shut up, not talking for a day was leading me into quite a difficult state of mind, and when I finally had the counselling I needed, it was a welcome release.

The counsellor used to be a midwife, and she was wonderful. Talking to someone about my experiences, being able to ask if I had done anything wrong during either pregnancy, really helped. Getting everything off my chest to a total stranger was what I needed. I had a lot of anger inside me, and I was so desperate for a baby that I'd become obsessed. Dave was nearly scared to come to bed!

June was SANDS Awareness Month, and throughout all of the above, Donna, my befriender, had been consistently supportive. She was hosting a balloon release to mark the month. It was a great opportunity to meet her and do something special for both Xander and Sausage. Meeting her and seeing so many other parents with their balloons really opened my eyes to how much this was happening. It was at that point that Dave and I decided that when we were ready, we wanted to become befrienders and help others like ourselves, as a couple. As we released the balloons, we also released a lot of our tears.

After a while of writing letters to Xander, I discovered a website called memory-of.com[16] and set up a page in memory. It was wonderful to be able to do something practical, adding photographs, songs, etc. Others were able to leave a tribute or light a candle, and I loved seeing that people had spent time visiting him. I visited regularly in the early days, then struggled especially when I felt I "needed" to get on for his anniversaries.

## One Year On

As the year progressed, I'd think "this time last year", wishing things could've been different. We made an area of our garden, Xander's area, which kept us busy and focused. I made a decision on the 1st September, that I was allowed a bad day, but on the 3rd September, I would celebrate his birthday and do things that I would've done had he been here; it would always be his day.

On the 3rd September, we took balloons and a message in a bottle down to the local beach. I wanted to do everything around the time he had been born. Unfortunately, I had not taken into consideration the tide. I had to walk forever in muddy sand to throw the message in the bottle

---

[16] Website is no longer available

into the sea. The problem was it kept coming back onto the mud, and I had to rescue it to try and make it go even further. As you can imagine, it wasn't easy, and I nearly fell on my rear end[17], making me giggle as I could just imagine Xander watching me and laughing.

## SANDS

In June 2006, Dave and I were put in touch with a group of SANDS Befrienders in Mid-Wales. Their Chairperson, Shirley, was organising an event for SANDS Awareness month and knew a few other mums from our area who were willing to help set up a group. To start, we'd need a Chair, Secretary and Treasurer. We were offered financial help with bereavement packs/boxes to supply to the hospital, attended training in Nottingham, where we met two ladies who were planning on setting up, so South Wales went from nothing to two groups at the same time, which was amazing.

The first day of SANDS training, I was both scared and excited. I'd never met so many other parents who had lost their babies before, and here we were, so many of us in the same room. There were dads, which was wonderful news for Dave. People brought together due to our loss and need to help others, to close friends. With our Befriender training passed, plans were put in place to hold our first meeting in October. We organised a balloon release event, and mum helped us secure facilities at the Road Safety Centre in Cardiff. Around eighty people turned up to release balloons, buy raffle tickets and remember their babies. It was a sad but wonderful launch, and the local paper covered it, so we had publicity about our meetings. With a secure meeting room, we were set to go. With the help of Mike's mum and the local Rotary Club, some fundraising through work, we raised enough money to refurbish a special suite at the local hospital. It was wonderful; it had a small sitting room with kitchen items, some toys, a TV and a DVD player. My parents donated a sofa bed so grandparents could stay with the parents, but at the same time give them space. A main bedroom was created for the parents with an ensuite bathroom. We put home comforts in, soft furnishings, an electric fan, a bath and a changing area so the family could spend more time together. Best of all, you couldn't hear a sound from outside the room. We opened the room on the 10th

---

[17] Colloquial British term for bottom

anniversary of Princess Diana's death, and we still made the lead story on the ITV news that night! We had a local radio DJ cut the ribbon and open the room for us, released more balloons and launched the tear drop sticker campaign, a sticker that would be put on mum's files to indicate they had a loss in a previous pregnancy. It was a wonderful day that went so well.

Representatives from work and the Rotary club attended, as well as parents from the group; some so brave returning to a hospital where they had lost their baby. Unfortunately, that room was closed just a few months after due to building work and a 'swap around'. The new room, although en-suite, is now open plan and next to the assessment unit, so now grieving parents have the pain of hearing heart monitors.

We soon started supporting the Royal Gwent Hospital, making us Cardiff & Newport SANDS. Shortly after, we began supporting the Royal Glamorgan Hospital, supplying bereavement rooms to all three hospitals that we look after, as well as cold and cuddle cots. All the things we never had when we lost Xander. I could write a separate book all about our events, our challenges, and some of our amazing parents and supporters. SANDS has been such a huge factor in my life.

Thanks to SANDS, I've experienced things I would never have done. Handing over a petition at the Welsh Assembly that had travelled from Snowdon to Cardiff by all means of transport, to being able to talk about Xander in the press. Attending an event at No. 10 Downing Street hosted by Samantha Cameron was an enormously proud day for me, and I thank Xander for that. He had become my motivation as well as my inspiration.

Trying for our third baby, I started worrying if it was ever going to happen for us. Attending SANDS meetings was becoming harder. Parents I'd supported were coming to meetings and announcing they were pregnant, and whilst I was genuinely pleased for them, I'd cry all the way home and for days, asking, "Why isn't it me?" with thoughts of, "I'm such a bad person; I don't deserve this chance". SANDS started to become a blessing and a curse, so I took a step back, only to be made redundant from a job I'd had for more than a decade. With the redundancy money I received, I changed direction to focus on what I wanted to do. Dave worked away a lot, so I started travelling with him. It was a wonderful experience, but also quite a lonely one. Applying for jobs, many I was overqualified for, was soul-destroying as I didn't get any interviews. My feeling of self-worth was extremely low, and I felt a failure in so many ways. Some days were very dark, and spending most of the day alone, I had plenty of time to think and shop. My redundancy money was going down very quickly, and I needed to decide what I wanted to do. I thought a counselling job would be the right thing, and I eventually got a job in the NHS Child Health Department as team leader. Being new to one of those questions I'd get asked was, "Have you got any children?" I decided to get it out of the way quite early on and explained the situation.

On the 10th Anniversary of Cardiff & Newport SANDS, we held our second ball. First, we gave tickets away, making it a thank-you and awareness event. With this second one, we were nearly sold out. We'd come so far in a few short years. On our way home on October 15th, my new little cousin Sofia arrived safely into the world, and as I stood outside Cardiff City Hall a few hours later, it turned pink and blue in support of Baby Loss Awareness Week. Social media was going mad over it. It would be an understatement to say I was a tad emotional that weekend.

## Muffin

Dave and I started talking about adoption. I wrote letters, put our names forward, but unfortunately, because of the new job I had, this was going to prove a little difficult. Then, after a few months working for the NHS, I discovered I was pregnant. Maybe because we'd started enjoying each other for the sake of enjoyment, and not making a baby, had helped. Everyone told us to relax, but when you crave a baby as much as I did, relaxing does not come easily. Even in your subconscious, you're still thinking, "Is this the time I will get pregnant?"

Happy to be pregnant again, and the first scan around Christmas, I couldn't wait to give the baby scan pictures as an extra present to our families on Christmas Day; finally, a good Christmas.

I felt different this time. Why would nature let us wait this long to spoil it for us? Unfortunately, I'd forgotten just how nasty nature could be.

Dave was away in Liverpool when I started spotting again. I was a mess; these poor work colleagues had only known me for two minutes, and there I was sobbing at my desk. My manager rang my dad, and it was time for another scan. Dave was home for the scan, and waiting in the baby unit to find out what was happening was such a horrible experience. It was so quiet everywhere, except in my head. Finally, I heard my name and headed for the dreaded internal scan. At seven weeks, the internal scan showed I was only four weeks. The baby wasn't growing. I was told it may be too early to say, but the fact that I was bleeding could mean that nature was running its course.

We were due to go to the Midlands that weekend, and it was pretty clear that I was miscarrying our long-awaited Muffin, a name we'd given her. My mum thought we should stay in Cardiff, but I argued that if this was going to happen, it would happen anywhere. The doctor said as long as I was close to a hospital, it would be okay if we went. I had no intention of going to a hospital. I knew what to expect, and I wasn't spending one night in a hospital losing another baby. I finished my Christmas shopping, and we spent the evening with family, who had no idea that my heart was breaking and how angry I was inside. They provided a welcome distraction that I needed badly.

We went back to the hospital on the 23rd of December, and the miscarriage was confirmed. Funny how we use the word lost isn't it, as I didn't leave the baby in the Midlands; my baby had died inside of me. I had so much anger inside of me, I felt someone had dangled a huge carrot in front of me, and then, as I got close to being excited, ripped it away from me and my heart.

On Boxing Day, Nicola told me that she was pregnant. She was going to be due two weeks after I would've been due. This meant I was going to watch another baby grow up the same age as mine. I was angry, and people, including Nicola, thought I was angry at her. I was so frustrated that no one, not even Dave, understood that I was not angry that people were getting on with life; I was angry that I was being denied doing so by nature. When you are angry, it is really hard to express your feelings correctly, and I know that at that time I upset a lot of people, which I never meant to do. Life just felt so very cruel to me.

# New Beginnings

My relationship with Dave had been suffering, and on his 40th Birthday, it felt even harder; even with SANDS, I had never felt so insecure. I hated going out alone, felt such a failure, had put on a lot of weight, and to make myself feel better, I spent money, which resulted in financial difficulty.

Dave and I always said we would talk to each other, but I found it increasingly difficult. I'd sit in SANDS meetings and ask other dads how they were coping, but I couldn't ask Dave. I was scared of his answers. I was carrying so much guilt that I still hadn't provided him with the child he so yearned for. Three times I'd become pregnant and three times I'd let him down. I knew that he didn't blame me, but I blamed myself, and that is hard to move past. I buried my head in the sand about our relationship and everything else going on around us. People close to me would tell me that he had changed and was starting to talk to me as though I was nothing, but I felt like I was nothing, so that was okay.

A week after our ninth wedding anniversary, Dave told me he was no longer in love with me. I cried for hours that night, but still didn't think he meant it or that he'd leave.

Dave moved in with his parents, and I thought my life was over. I was on the verge of forty, no living children and now no husband. Who would want me at my age? I thought my future was bleak. I didn't love myself, so who would? It took a few nights of being alone and awake all night to realise that I was stronger than the person I was being, I'd lost sight of who I truly was, and that to move forward, I needed to find her again.

Realising I needed to move forward, I started having fun again and building up my confidence. I started seeing someone, and my confidence started to grow again. Dave wanted to talk about getting back together. We tried, but unfortunately, just before Xander's 17th Birthday, we separated for good. During the split on Christmas Day that year, I reached my lowest point and sat in the bath with a knife, deciding that it would be best for everyone if I were no longer here, and

I wanted to be with my children. As I sat crying, holding that knife, my phone rang, and a special person reminded me that I would see my children, but not yet. He saved me that night.

Thanks to therapy, I realised that whilst Dave and I will always love each other, we were no longer *in* love with each other. We're both moving forward with our lives. It is so important that if you're going through anything like this, you need to talk with each other. Dave and I failed to do that for a second time as we did not learn from the first time, and we were, and still are, in quite different places with our grief for Xander.

We've celebrated Xander's Angelversary and birthdays in many different ways over the years, but one constant has been family. For some reason, the 10th Angelversary hit me hard, and I thought it may have been because I hadn't moved on with living children. Sometimes grief has no rhyme or reason; it can just catch you when you least expect it.

The SANDS Welsh Network Co-Ordinator was stepping down, and they were advertising for the role. It was the last thing I wanted to do, even though I was very passionate about the work. After a Lights of Love service, I was persuaded to apply as a volunteer. I took on the role, and over time, it became a paid position. I needed to attend various meetings with the Welsh Government, so I gave up working for the NHS to concentrate on SANDS full-time.

I used to wonder what I wanted to be when I grew up, but I never thought this would be my dream job. I love it, though. I'm making a difference to so many parents who've walked in my shoes. I work with amazing people, and my job is so varied. One day, I am being interviewed for a news report, and the next, I can be in a cemetery looking at an area suitable for a new baby garden and discussing cremations. I feel out of my depth in discussions when trained medical staff talk about things I've not been trained in. Often, I need a dictionary when I get home to work out the conversation. It is a challenging role, and people often ask me how I can deal with the subject of baby loss daily, but I live with the reality of baby loss every day, only now I give hope to others.

SANDS Wales has grown a lot, and the volunteers who give up their time to support parents are amazing. Becoming a trainer for Sands is a job that I love so much, and between the two roles, life is very varied. I was furloughed during COVID, as were many of my colleagues. Shortly afterwards, several redundancies happened and close colleagues moved on to pastures new. It was a very unsettling and upsetting time. I was safe in my role, and I felt guilty and relieved; it was a time of mixed emotions. Thankfully and gratefully, I'm still good friends with those amazing ladies in my life.

# Jax

Whilst Dave and I were together, we got a dog, even though I resisted; I eventually ran out of excuses. I wanted a small one that didn't shed and one that didn't smell when wet. I'd grown up terrified of dogs, but started looking at a website called Many Tears Rescue Centre. I fell in love with a litter that had been born to a mum who'd been rescued when pregnant. Mum was a Border Collie, and the six pups were a crossbreed. Not what I had thought I was looking for, but when I saw the little face looking back at me on the computer of a six-week-old pup called Frost, I knew he was mine.

Adopting a puppy is hard work, and I understand why people buy one. I had to provide a letter from my employer proving that I worked from home. We received a home visit to check that we were suitable, and on the 8th November 2017, we became the proud human parents of Frost. I spent the morning of the ninth running around to pick up all the essentials and put a little teddy bear into the pet carrier. Our fur baby was the last to go; the mum had already been adopted, and his five siblings were all over the place.

Meeting Frost for the first time, I knew it was going to be perfect. I did the paperwork whilst Dave had lots of cuddles. We named our new pup Jax after the main character of Sons of Anarchy, and as we drove off, he started crying and trying to get out of the carrier. Anarchy right there! Dave told me to take him out and hold him, but I'd always avoided holding animals; I didn't have a clue what I was doing. I unzipped the carrier and awkwardly lifted him out, put him on my lap and told him it was going to be okay. As I stroked him, he stopped crying and fell asleep in my arms.

He slept all night and was great in the car. Toilet training took a while, and we had a few issues with chewing. I felt I'd made a mistake at one point after he had been playing outside for ages, and then came in and urinated right next to me and not on the puppy pad. I locked myself in the toilet and cried. Dave was constantly worried in the early days that I would change my mind and take Jax back to the pound, but I wasn't giving up that easily. I wouldn't be able to send a baby back, and I wasn't going to send my dog back.

Jax makes me laugh, frustrates me, makes me cry and makes my heart ooze with love. I was terrified of losing him or something happening to him, and my anxiety and panic attacks started to flare up again, something I hadn't had for a few years. I was constantly crying over silly things, and my mood swings were awful. One minute I would be okay, and then I would feel so low. Panic attacks came on if too many people were around me, and I got to the point where I was terrified of going somewhere new. It was hard to explain it, so I took part in a six-week anxiety and depression course. The early morning walks with Jax were so therapeutic.

I'd never understood people's relationships with their dogs and how they treated them as their children, but now I do. Having Jax as a puppy and watching him grow has helped my confidence, not only with dogs but with animals in general. I've been able to feed horses and walk with all different breeds. If anyone had told me I would be feeding treats to Rottweilers, German Shepherds, Labradors and holding not one but four puppies at a time, I would have said you were mental! I love Jax as if he were my baby, and it terrifies me knowing that I will outlive another child and will have to say goodbye and bury him. I'm hoping that is a long way off, as he is so precious to me.

## Eighteen Years

After eighteen years, people expect you to have moved on and gotten over 'it', hence the title of this chapter, "Are you better yet?" It is a prime example of someone trying to say something, but not feeling comfortable with the silence and getting it wrong. If you don't know what to say to a bereaved parent, tell them you are sorry that you've no idea what to say. Telling someone they are still young enough to have more when you have no idea if they can does not make them feel better.

It took a while for me to believe that my son would have been turning eighteen. I didn't feel any older, and it made me wonder what he'd look like, what he'd be like, what his interests would've been and the type of man he would've become. For many years, I struggled to be around Kaden as I missed Xander and needed cognitive therapy. The therapist told me that whatever Kaden was doing, think of Xander doing the opposite. It has helped over the years.

My fundraising efforts continued with a darts tournament, a sponsored dog walk and a party, which saw over £700 raised for Sands and over £550 for Pancreatic Cancer.

I wanted Xander's name to travel the world because I thought I'd teach Xander about the world, but instead, I have taught the world about him. Asking friends and family to 'take him with them' on their travels, celebrating his name in some way, meant his name touched as many places as possible. So many people helped, and thanks to a lovely lady, I was introduced to a Facebook page where people exchange notes. I do one for them here, and they do one for me wherever they live. I have met some amazing people and learnt so much. People have gone above and beyond, which has shown me how beautiful people can be. I emailed a restaurant in America called Dangerfield's and asked them if they would put Xander's name in front of the restaurant, and they did so much more! They put a poster together saying, "Happy birthday, Xander!" and in memory of his birthday, they offered a free meal to anyone sharing his birthday week. This blew me away; although due to how the Americans write dates, there was a slight confusion and free meals were given away on the 9th March instead, which I thought was hilarious, as that was Xander's grandma's birthday. I thought it was quite fitting.

Learning that you can't look at the what-ifs, only look at the future, has been so necessary. People have asked me over the years what has helped me cope; psychics have been one thing, family another. My SANDS family has been a huge part of it, and finding and being comfortable with the new me. That last bit has been the hardest. There are days that

I feel I'm making progress and days when I feel enormous guilt for everything that my family doesn't have, especially Dave. I've robbed him of so much: children, a home of our own and his future. Logical days tell me that not all of it was my fault.

I kept the faith that I'd have more children, but I'm now fairly sure I'm in menopause, so it is looking highly unlikely. Part of me is not even sure how I'd react if a miracle did happen. The realisation that I'll never see my child graduate, get married, have children, or grow old is a harsh one. There's also the thought of when I'm gone, who'll continue telling his story and keeping his memory alive, but also who will I leave special mementoes to? You just assume when you are younger that you will have children and that everything you have will one day be theirs. That everything you do in life is about creating a future for them. It's a sobering thought when you realise you don't have that, and will never have grandchildren or great-grandchildren. As we get older and my friends become grandparents, it brings it even more to life.

As an only child, I feel guilty that I've not given my parents grandchildren to spoil rotten in their retirement, as I know they are so desperate to do. They have to listen to their friends and siblings talk about their grandchildren and great-grandchildren, knowing they can never fully join in the conversation. I also live with the guilt that my husband is the only boy, and his surname will die with him. I feel guilty that I stopped Dave from becoming a dad to a living baby. Part of me wishes that whilst we had split, he'd met a lovely lady and had a family. I feel I have stopped him from having so much.

Without family members, I'd never have experienced visits to Santa, school concerts, nativity plays and school sports days. Simple things which seem so normal to most people, but are so precious to me. Receiving Mother's Day cards from Kaden made me cry, but they still have such a special meaning to me.

Dave and I are now focusing on life apart, not what could have been; it has taken a long time to get to this stage. Losing a child is a life-changing experience, and going on to realise you will never have a living child is an even harder burden, but I'm here to tell the story that you can survive. Seek help when and where you need it; it is more of a weakness not getting it than having it.

## Women I'm Inspired By

Katherine Johnson (NASA) - this woman was amazing, she was a genius in a man's world who not only had to fight to be heard because she was a woman but also had to fight harder because she was a black woman. She endured so much but finally was heard and prospered, inspiring women everywhere.

The women in my family are all inspiring, from my great gran who being a Polish Jew fled an abusive, arranged marriage, married my great grandad and was discovered as a bigamist and gave birth to her first born in prison. She brought up 12 children in difficult times, losing a son in the war. My mum had me at 18, she went back to study in her early 30s, nursed my nan with cancer until she died, looked after my grampy losing him just 6 months after her first grandchild had died and just days before her 50th. Shortly after my dad was diagnosed with prostate cancer and I had a further miscarriage. She's supported me and been my rock as have all my family. A family of mainly women, we have all gone through many obstacles but have overcome as a family, pulling together from each other's strength.

# Reflections

# Reflections

## Neeve Fleurette Andrews
## South Africa

Neeve, affectionately known as Nevil, is the determined founder of South Africa's first Primary Animal Health Care Facility, Nevils Animal Care. In 2023, Nevil launched her groundbreaking facility, quickly gaining recognition in the animal health community. Her work was featured in an article by the African Advanced Academy and an interview with Farm Radio International.

Through her efforts, she aims to inspire and empower women across Africa to take on leadership roles in the traditionally male-dominated animal industry, advocating for greater representation and equality. With her tenacity and compassion, Nevil is making a significant impact on the lives of animals and paving the way for future generations of women in the field.

Her bond with animals is profound, rooted in understanding and empathy. This ability enriches her life and fuels her dedication to her work. In her leisure time, she enjoys nature through activities like fishing and hiking, seeking refuge from her professional demands. She navigates life's complexities with dark humour, using laughter as a coping mechanism.

Nevil balances her career with a loving relationship with her fiancé. They share their home with four playful cats and a loyal dog, creating a nurturing environment that reflects their shared love for animals.

https://nevilsanimalcare.com
Facebook: https://facebook.com/nevilsanimalcare

# Nevil.

I often find myself at a loss for where to commence, particularly when life's tapestry is woven with such intricate threads and condensing it into a mere few thousand words feels daunting. It's akin to the initial moments of a therapy session, where the therapist prompts you to unveil your essence.
"Well, I'm Neeve."

In that moment, you can't help but feel as though you've stepped into an AA or NA gathering, where the group resonates in unison, "Hi Neeeeve," their voices steeped in warmth. And thus, the adventure begins.

I stand as the proud founder, CEO and Veterinary Technician of Nevil's Animal Care, a beacon of hope in South Africa, where I have ventured to establish the very first Primary Animal Health Care Facility. This journey required immense courage and resilience, as I transitioned from a steady salary to embrace the unknown of entrepreneurship, stepping into an industry where I was but a stranger. Undoubtedly, this leap was the second most daunting experience of my life, yet I am profoundly grateful for it, for I shall never glance back nor retreat to my former path. I firmly hold that when the shadows of fear loom over a new beginning, one should embrace that emotion and cultivate it into a force of great potential.

My animal health venture is a mobile enterprise, born from the realisation of a market void where many around me struggled to transport their cherished pets to the veterinarian. Some, having sold their cars while working from home, faced challenges in seeking care for their furry companions. In a world where the hustle of work often overshadows personal needs, I sought to ease this burden, providing a more convenient and less stressful solution for pets by bringing animal health care directly to their doorstep. Home is where the heart dwells, a sanctuary of love and comfort; why should that serenity be disrupted for both animals and their devoted owners?

Awakening each day is a cherished gift. Who wouldn't yearn to spend their life surrounded by the enchanting presence of animals? Each day unfolds with promise... save for those moments when a joyous pup showers your shoe with their exuberance. The squelching sound of a slightly fragrant golden liquid between your toes can be quite the surprise! Yet, even in that amusing misadventure, a heart brimming with joy prevails, for I am blessed to work with these delightful creatures every day. This always stirs memories of university practicals, where we journeyed from the charming companionship of small animals, such as cats and dogs, to the grander realms of domestic creatures like cows and pigs. Among our lessons was the intricate study of male pigs' reproductive organs and the wonders of AI (Artificial Insemination). I shall spare you the elaborate details, but to weave the tale briefly: during one memorable session, the bull's sperm met an unexpected trajectory and landed squarely in my left eyeball! Laughter erupted, etching this moment into our hearts, a whimsical memory that forever lingers, never to deter my passion for this vocation. Animals have always been my true calling, and not even the most humorous mishaps can sway me from my love for them.

I must share the truth: three incredibly important souls grace my life, standing steadfast before and throughout the trials I've faced. My fiancée, my sister, and my brother-in-law, without their unwavering support, I doubt I would have traversed my path as swiftly. While I know I would have eventually leapt toward my fears, the journey would have been far lengthier. There were moments when I felt ensnared between a rock and a hard place, yet they became my pillars, the very foundation upon which a greater version of myself was built.

They imparted a profound lesson: it's perfectly acceptable not to always feel okay. It is okay to shed tears, to walk away from places that bring discontent, and to pursue joy instead of merely pleasing others. Not everyone will resonate with you, and that's entirely acceptable. Embrace what brings you happiness because life is far too fleeting to do otherwise.

The path I have traversed to reach my current station has been nothing short of a formidable odyssey. Confronted by envious rivals and uninformed onlookers who simply failed to grasp the essence of my craft, I have faced a multitude of voices seeking to undermine my spirit. They have proclaimed that I shall never succeed, that my endeavours are beyond the pale of legality, and that my character is flawed. While I recognise that we all encounter our fair share of "Karens" along the way, I can only marvel at the sheer magnitude of the 'Karens' I have met (perhaps I was one in a past life to warrant such vitriol from so many). When a fire ignites within, your emotions soar to exhilarating heights... ceaselessly! Thus, I find myself compelled to express gratitude to those who, in silence, shaped my journey, thank you! Your contributions have fortified my spirit and taught me the art of transforming negativity into a mere whisper, easily cast aside.

A myriad of delightful experiences have accompanied my venture onto this new path. I had the honour of being sponsored by the FAO (Food and Agriculture Organisation) to present at the World Veterinary Association Congress in the vibrant city of Cape Town, South Africa. This opportunity allowed me to showcase my business while guiding fellow associates in the art of launching enterprises akin to mine. I had the honour of being interviewed by Farm Radio International, leading to a beautifully crafted article by the African Advanced Academy, celebrating the empowerment of women. Though shadows linger in our world, I have truly discovered the art of transforming the dark into light, nurturing the flames of positivity, the radiant fire that ignites hope.

Allow me to guide you back to the genesis of my journey. At the tender age of six, I discovered my profound adoration for animals. I believe that every child possesses a natural affinity for these creatures, for their spirits resonate with our own. Yet, to uncover a love infused with passion is a rare treasure. Typically, I remain ensconced in my solitude when reflecting on my life's trials, especially the darker moments. However, I have come to realise that stifling these emotions has not nurtured my spirit; instead, it has begun to transform me, and such change should only be for the betterment of oneself. Thus, here I stand, baring my soul to the universe (quite literally). As I pen this heartfelt passage, my hands tremble, tears cascade down my cheeks, and I can sense my heartbeat echoing in my throat. Yet, I know this act of vulnerability holds the key to my healing... It is imperative.

I hail from a tapestry woven with complexity... Two brothers, two sisters, and, naturally, a mother and father grace my lineage. One brother is my twin, while my other siblings are my half-sisters and brother. The sister closest to my heart, Rex, is eleven years my senior. In those formative years, she was my sole sister, and together we navigated the tempest of life. Though sisters may clash over borrowed clothes or pilfered makeup, our bond transcends such trivial squabbles, forged through trials that have united us like no other. We share a different father yet the same mother, and yet my sister has been a guiding light, a maternal figure more profound than my mother. Her influence has sculpted me into the strong, empowered woman I am today.

My father, oh, how it saddens me to utter that title, a true embodiment of monstrosity. The earliest recollection I possess of my father dates back to when I was around five or six years of age. As I strolled through the corridor of the TV room, I made my way upstairs to my haven, returning home from the day's school adventures, and he emerged from the shadows, seizing me with a force that struck like thunder (again and again). In mere moments, my lower back, behind, and legs transformed into a canvas of black and blue hues. To sit, lie down, or even walk was a torment, yet I held my silence close, shrouded in fear. I distinctly remember rising with the dawn, ensuring I bathed early, desperate to shield my mother and sister from the truth of my wounds. The thought of them discovering my plight filled me with dread, for I feared my father's wrath would rain down upon them should they dare to speak. Alas, fate had other plans, and one fateful day, my mother entered as I changed after bathing, her eyes falling upon the bruises that told a silent, sorrowful tale.

I recall her confronting him, but the aftermath was a stillness that echoed louder than words, no embrace, no glimmer of solace. Alone in my room, tears flowed freely, and in that moment of despair, a gentle spirit entered: one of our dogs, a Weimaraner named Crystal. She nestled beside me, offering a warmth I craved more than any human comfort. I clung to her tightly, finding solace in her presence, feeling both heartbroken and grateful that a dog could offer me the love I longed for. Crystal, at around four years of age, became the beacon of hope and clarity in my darkest hours. In her eyes, I glimpsed my true calling, a passion ignited within me to become a veterinarian, dedicated to rescuing animals just as she had rescued me.

My father, in a few poignant words, embodies the shadows of a drunkard, an alcoholic, an abuser, and a narcissist, what the modern world might call a gas lighter. Countless nights, he would succumb to the bottle, staggering into his car, only for us to receive late-night calls, his voice slurred, beckoning my mother to rescue him from the wreckage of his choices. On other occasions, the guardians of our estate would return him to our doorstep, a reminder of his chaotic existence. As I grapple with the weight of my feelings, I often wish he were the kind of father who ventured out for milk, never to return. Yet, in my tender youth, I adored him fiercely, living in fear of the day I might receive that dreadful call, informing me of his demise in a tragic car accident.

My father soared through the skies as a pilot, possessing his own fleet of aircraft and occasionally sharing the skies with others. He dazzled crowds at Air Shows, performing breathtaking stunts, flipping upside down and twirling through the heavens. Our family escapades often took to the clouds for our holidays, one would think pride, gratitude, and excitement would abound, yet I felt none. Instead, a tempest of fear gripped me before each flight, knowing he had indulged in drink the night prior, a perilous choice akin to driving under the influence. The anticipation would churn my stomach, and my aversion to flying grew, casting a shadow on my thoughts about planes and the entire aviation realm.

We would soar with him to all his thrilling airshows, yet there was one particular event from which we refrained. I was about eighteen years old, standing at the threshold of my final school year. Just hours before our departure, my beloved dog, Crystal, suffered a heart attack. Another family ascended aboard my father's six-seater plane, which was meant to carry us, while he piloted a smaller two-seater. My mother made the heart-wrenching decision to cancel our trip so we could remain by Crystal's side, and tragically, that plane met its fate in a crash, leaving no survivors. On that fateful day, Crystal also departed from this world. It felt as though my entire universe crumbled. She remains the spark that ignites my passion.

In the tender realms of my youth, my mother, in my eyes, was the epitome of motherhood. I sensed her boundless love for all of us, yet that was merely the surface. As I ventured into the tapestry of life, maturing and awakening to her true essence, both past and present, I felt the need to step back from our bond, allowing time to heal and to unravel the complexities of our shared journey.

My mother, as illuminated by my therapist in our recent sessions, appears to grapple with a Cluster B Personality Disorder, one that diminishes the spirits of women stronger than herself, particularly her own daughters. She struggles to celebrate my successes and feels even more disdain knowing I have a partner who embodies qualities she once lacked. Rather than bask in pride for my accomplishments, she seeks to cast shadows over my life, proclaiming to the world what a terrible person I am. The light of my virtues remains unseen by her eyes, as she finds solace in my struggles, relishing in my pain. Yet here I stand today, resilient and empowered, rising above the emotional storms she continues to unleash.

My mother once shared two haunting tales from my infancy, recounting a moment when she discovered our father looming over my twin and me, attempting to stifle our breaths with a pillow while we peacefully slumbered in our cot, and yet another tale where my father pursued her and my siblings through our garden, a gun in hand. I was merely seven years old when this revelation unfolded, and the circumstances of that conversation linger in the shadows of my mind.

At the time, I thought, "What a burden it must have been to live with such a man; I can only imagine the fear she must have felt." Yet now, as the sands of time have shifted, I find myself bewildered. Who divulges such a chilling truth to a child? Why did I feel compassion for her instead of terror? After hearing those words, I still returned home and embraced my father. WHY!? Countless questions lie buried within me, waiting to be unearthed.

I find myself shying away from the terms dad, father, or any paternal name, as they send shivers down my spine, those of discomfort, not delight. When I speak of him, I always invoke his name, for in my heart, he is no longer my dad. A true dad embodies a protector, a mentor, and a steadfast supporter; he is the one who lifts you when you stumble, brushes you off, and encourages you to rise anew. A father is cherished and revered, often hailed as a son's first hero and a daughter's inaugural love, an embodiment of a real-life Superman. Alas, this has not been the reality for me or my siblings. As the sands of time slipped through our fingers, the shadows of abuse deepened, physically, mentally, and verbally. He succumbed to the grasp of alcoholism, and that dark descent amplified the turmoil a hundredfold. His drink of choice? Whiskey, Johnny Walker Black on the rocks, a generous pour when the coin allowed. Otherwise, it was the humbler Johnny Walker Red. And then, as the evening unfolded, he would indulge in not just a glass or two, but three, or four... perhaps even the entire bottle of wine alongside his meal. It goes without saying that he never took it upon himself to prepare dinner; if the feast was not ready when his hunger struck, the only option was to run, run far away. Better yet, flee to your car and drive as fast as the wind would carry you.

I remember those chaotic moments vividly, plates, knives, forks, and glasses hurled through the air; a tempest of fury unleashed because dinner was delayed. Doors slammed, gates rattled, and walls bore the brunt of his wrath. And if we happened to be caught in the storm? Well, you can imagine the consequences. He would resolutely refuse to consume anything at all, holding out until we all surrendered to slumber. The descent into sleep was fraught with trepidation, each moment laced with the uncertainty of what awaited us. I recall the shadowy trek downstairs to quench my thirst, only to glimpse him feasting in the darkness, accompanied by his bottle of wine. He caught sight of me and bellowed, "BED! NOW!" All I sought was a simple glass of water and expressed my wish - yet, in return, I received a few sharp smacks and was banished to my chamber. That night, I lay awake, yearning for his slumber to embrace me, but instead, I was met with unsettling sounds as he settled into his own room. I emerged from the cocoon of my bed and tiptoed to my parents' chamber, only to behold a nightmarish scene etched forever in my memory... his hands encircling my mother's throat. Panic surged through me as I dashed downstairs, seized the baseball bat hidden behind our front door, and raced back upstairs, determined to confront him, and declare that he must leave my mother be, or face the consequences. I don't believe I have ever trembled so profoundly in my existence; the quiver resonated in my voice and echoed in my breath. He cast her upon the bed and declared, "Okay. I see how this is.," He grasped his house keys and car keys tightly, and just before he thundered the front door shut, he shouted, "Fuck all of you, you can rot in fucking hell." He slipped into his BMW, a tempest of speed and fury, spinning his tyres as he vanished into the night. I recall the warmth of my mother's embrace, as I whispered assurances that everything would be all right, I must have been around eleven years old then. I brewed her some tea, gently tucked her into bed, and watched over her as she drifted into slumber, the baseball bat hidden beneath the duvet, a silent guardian.

Awakened by his presence the next morning, I found my mother still lost in dreams. He seized my arm, propelling me from the sanctuary of her room, slamming the bedroom door behind us, his breath reeking of a distillery. His grip was so fierce that by the next day, a black and purple bruise blossomed across my forearm. My sister was absent at that time, but I ventured into her sanctuary, hoping to use her makeup to conceal the mark; alas, my efforts proved futile, compelling me to don a long t-shirt even under the sweltering sun of summer. I cannot summon the memories of that fateful morning, the moment he thrust me out of the room. What lingers is the eerie silence, a haunting presence far more terrifying than any shout, leaving me adrift in uncertainty. Then, as if summoned by fate, my mother emerged, clad and resolute, ushering us forth to school. Like a whisper lost in the winds, the silence enveloped me; not a word graced my ears that day, nor the one that followed, as everything was simply swept beneath the carpet. I inquired about her well-being during our drive to school, and all she could muster was, "I'm good, Nuu." Nunu, a tender moniker bestowed upon me by my mother, resonated in the air. I sat in quiet contemplation, my mind swirling with questions: How? How is she truly well? Why has no discussion unfolded? Why do we continue as if all is normal, and why does my father linger still?

My sister, Rex, was often immersed in her studies or spending weekends at her partner's abode. Yet, upon her return home, it seemed my father harboured an inexplicable disdain for her. This perplexing riddle has lingered in my mind, a mystery I continue to unravel even now. As my twin and I approached the tender age of twelve, the sands of time ushered in a new chapter: we no longer shared a sanctuary. I found myself in the company of Rex, while my twin took refuge with our elder brother. In this new arrangement, sharing a room with my sister unveiled shadows from the past, echoes of my father's actions that had haunted her. Being the elder, she bore the weight of the turmoil, enduring the brunt of his cruelty. I recall those nights when, just before surrendering to slumber, my sister would perch upon her bed, immersed in her studies. As I drifted into dreams, I would occasionally awaken to the harsh echoes of our father's cruel words directed at her. In those moments, I chose to feign sleep, gripped by fear that if I stirred, he might turn his ire upon me, leaving me powerless to shield her from his wrath. While cloaked in the guise of slumber, I listened as he berated her about her then-boyfriend, deeming him pathetic and insisting she sever ties with him. With a sudden surge of fury, he seized her phone, rifling through her messages. In a moment of reckless abandon, he hurled the device against the wall, shattering it into countless fragments. He would persistently employ his index finger, pushing and prodding her chest with such force that the rhythmic thump of his touch echoed in the air. He frequently seized her by the arms, tossing her clothes from the cupboard, commanding her to fuck off to her then-beloved. In the shadowy echoes of countless moments, there came a night when he seized her, thrusting her into the cupboard while his hands constricted around her throat. My heart raced, yearning to leap from the bed and come to her aid, yet my body betrayed me, paralysed by a shroud of cowardice. Was it fear that held me captive? As he finally departed the room, I sprang up and enveloped my sister in a fierce embrace, vowing never to let her slip away. With whispered apologies and declarations of unwavering support, I nestled into her bed, trembling at the thought of his return, too frightened to part from her side. My sister stood as a steadfast guardian of our family, willingly absorbing the storms of hardship to shield her siblings from their fury. She was the superhero of our humble abode.

Every week, a new shadow was unveiled, as I lived in the unsettling rhythm of fear under my father's roof. When he returned home, I would dash to my beloved dogs, seeking solace in their playful spirits, holding them close in a desperate bid for comfort. His drinking spiralled into a haze so profound that he often awoke with no memory of the chaos he had wrought. Denial dripped from his lips like poison; he would refute the anguish he inflicted upon us, deny his betrayals of my mother, and even claim he hadn't indulged in the bottle at all.

One fateful weekend, I ventured to a friend's house, where the thrill of quad biking in the veld turned treacherous. An accident sent the bike tumbling down a hill, pinning me beneath it, leaving me with burns and grazes. When I returned home, my mother tended to my wounds, bathing me gently before tucking me into bed. But tranquillity was shattered when my drunken father stormed in, his voice a tempest as he hurled accusations at my mother: "THIS IS YOUR FAULT! GET TO THE ROOM!" In that moment of chaos, Crystal, our loyal dog, burst into the fray, positioning herself protectively between my mother and us, barking fiercely at my father. In a fit of rage, he seized Crystal, kicking her as she yelped in terror. My heart roared with fury as I screamed for him to stop. He then dragged my mother away, leaving Crystal trembling on the floor. I rushed to her, enveloping her in a tight embrace, checking her over before guiding her to her bed, covering her with love. Throughout our lives, we have welcomed countless dogs, each one a cherished companion, despite the shadows cast by his drinking. Each memory lingers, etched in time; every dog remains unforgettable, each bestowing upon me a profound purpose to persevere through life's trials.

With dread clutching my throat, I entered my parents' room, only to find my sister struggling to fend off our father's wrath. Panic surged within me as I shouted in horror. In that moment, I confronted him with trembling resolve, declaring my hatred and the promise of calling the authorities if he did not leave. That night, he stormed off, leaving with only a bag, and did not return until Monday evening. In a moment suspended in time, my mother embraced him with open, loving arms... Excuse me? A wave of confusion washed over me, and I pondered: perhaps they had spoken and reconciled? Could their love be that profound? Reflecting on it now as an adult, the shadows of these memories loom large, why did my mother never choose to leave him? Why did she endure the torrents of abuse? Why did she allow her children to suffer? The beloved dogs, too, why did she permit their mistreatment? How could she continue to love him while sweeping the darkness of abuse beneath the rug?

At the tender age of seventeen, a new chapter unfolded as my sister and I embraced the gift of our own rooms, thanks to our elder brother's departure. To a dwelling closer to the university, Rex would occasionally grace us with her presence during the week, yet the weekends were when she truly returned. As I navigated the tumultuous waters of my final school examinations, my father seemed determined to disrupt the fragile peace of our studies. I can still recall those moments vividly. In my quest for solitude, I would shut my door, only for him to ascend the stairs, unlock it, and decree that I must study with the door ajar, and then, with a flourish, he would hurl my books across the room. He would then retreat to the living room, turning the music to such a volume that the very windows trembled in response. Amidst this cacophony, he would indulge in drink, and I understood that I needed to remain alert, ever watchful to protect my mother and the animals.

High school proved to be an arduous journey for me, and I emerged with merely average marks, largely due to the formidable challenges my father imposed on my studies. Just three nights before my pivotal matric biology exam, a tempest of conflict erupted between my parents, culminating in my mother suffering a heart attack. To my astonishment, it was my father who rushed her to the hospital that night, where she was admitted to the ICU, stabilised but fragile. The following day, he took my twin and me to school, only to deliver the harrowing news three hours later: our brother was en route to fetch us, for our mother's life hung in the balance. What kind of person conveys such grim tidings to their children? Why not offer solace and hope, especially during such a critical time?

Miraculously, my mother survived, her doctors informing us that only 60% of her heart was functioning, requiring her to rely on medication for the rest of her life. Regrettably, my finals suffered as a consequence; I passed, but not with the straight A's I had aspired to achieve. This led me down a dark path, engulfed in anger and despair, knowing that my dreams of attending Onderstepoort, the sole university for Veterinary Science in South Africa, were slipping further from my grasp. In the twilight of my school years, I encountered a dog named Indigo, a serendipitous rescue that felt like destiny, love at first sight. It was as if she had known me all along. At three years old, she bounded into my life, racing straight to my room, instantly claiming her space. Fiercer than Crystal, she became my steadfast guardian. Whenever my father would indulge in drink, Indigo would promptly settle by my feet, offering solace, and I would brace myself for what was to come.

As my father attempted to reach for her, she would growl protectively, a fierce warning that led to her suffering. Each time he retaliated against her, I intervened, but there came a moment when he seized my arm and cast me to the floor, intent on continuing his cruelty. Indigo became my unwavering shadow, an embodiment of loyalty in my life.

I forged ahead and submitted my application to the university. The forms presented two pathways, should the first falter. Yet, I mused, I had no alternative, for Veterinary Science was the very essence of my passion. Thus, I embraced my heart's desire and listed solely the BVSc (Bachelor of Veterinary Science). Despite my fervent hopes, the response was a denial. Words fail to capture the depths of my despair, uselessness, anger, depression, and demotivation washed over me. In that moment, I questioned the purpose of existence if I could not pursue my true calling. When I faced rejection from Onderstepoort for Veterinary studies, it was Indigo who illuminated my path through that suffocating darkness; she breathed hope into my weary soul. I shall eternally owe her a debt of gratitude. Surrendering was not an option; I couldn't yield when every cherished animal in my life had been a beacon of support through my emotional trials. So, I embarked on a quest, searching, searching, searching. At last, I discovered an undergraduate course in Animal Health offered by the University of South Africa (UNISA), a path that allowed me to study while working.

This meant I could finance my education independently, as neither my father nor my mother could provide that support.

With fervour igniting my spirit, I swiftly applied and was welcomed into the fold. My heart danced with joy as I thought, "YES! This is my gateway into the realm of Veterinary medicine." I embraced a role as an Au Pair, which offered a commendable salary, enough to sustain my car, studies, and fuel for my journey. After two years of nurturing young souls, I yearned for a deeper experience and sought a position at a veterinary clinic to further my aspirations. My initial salary of R800 per month reflected my weekend-only hours, but fortune smiled upon me as the vet recognised my dedication and promoted me. Soon, I was immersed in work from Monday to Saturday while juggling my studies.

For three fulfilling years, I devoted myself to this practice before daring to apply once more. Graduating with cum laude honours, I presented my application fortified with glowing recommendations from esteemed Veterinarians and mentors who had guided me through my journey. Yet, to my dismay, I faced rejection once again. My heart sank; I had toiled endlessly for my Animal Health Diploma. But this setback did not extinguish my resolve. Surely, there must be a path forward. Why is the journey so arduous? My passion runs deep; I have dedicated myself to the study of animals and have been immersed in the industry for six years. I have proudly unveiled the very FIRST Primary Animal Health Care Facility in South Africa. What more must I offer to Onderstepoort?

It weighs heavily on my heart that they often see only a number, overlooking the essence of individual stories and passions. It pains me to witness the waning fervour within South Africa's veterinary landscape. Yet, I shall not waver. My commitment remains steadfast, for I will never give up.

It has taken me a considerable journey to pen these thoughts, filled with tears and the weight of worries about how others may perceive me. Particularly those who know me well, who I trust will purchase this book in solidarity, yet remain unaware of the depths of my past, as I have seldom shared it. I once held the belief that revealing one's past was a sign of weakness or a call for attention. However, the act of inscribing even a fragment of my life has proven to be a balm for my soul, guiding me toward healing.

The most profound memory that ensnares my emotions and urges me to retreat into shadows is the day I faced the choice of abortion. It followed the heart-wrenching news of my rejection from Onderstepoort, the solitary institution in South Africa where one can pursue veterinary studies. In that moment of despair, I lost my way, forging connections with a tumultuous crowd who danced with danger, indulging in substances as their highs faded into oblivion. These were souls entwined with gangs and the underbelly of drug lords. Our nights were a whirlwind of clubbing and bar-hopping, from Monday through Sunday. Yet, amidst the chaos, I remained untouched by drugs, though the bottle became my companion, leading me deeper into the abyss of depression. I neglected my well-being, shedding pounds and distancing myself from cherished friendships, vanishing from the lives of those who cared.

When the news of my pregnancy arrived, it marked a pivotal turn in my destiny. Fear gripped me, for I was only seven weeks along, anxious for both my life and that of the fragile new existence within. The choice to terminate the pregnancy weighed heavily on my heart, influenced by the tumultuous life I was entwined with. I could not bear to usher a soul into a world marred by drugs, alcohol, despair, and abuse.

In the midst of this turmoil, I reached out to my sister, pouring my heart out. She listened intently, ensuring I was resolute in my decision, while also assuring me that, regardless of the path I chose, she and her husband would stand unwaveringly by my side through every twist and turn. I reflect upon this daily, acutely aware of the countless women who face the heartache of infertility. My sister, a beacon of hope, has been blessed with conception through IVF three times, yet her journey has been fraught with trials that weigh heavily on my heart, filling me with a sense of guilt for my own choices.

When my sister planned a holiday with her family, she graciously offered her home as a refuge during my difficult time. I ventured to a nearby clinic, where I was given two sets of tablets, which I took as soon as I arrived at her abode. The pain that followed was unimaginable, as if my very essence was being torn apart; no painkiller could dull the agony that engulfed me.

The ordeal of the abortion, compounded by rejection from Onderstepoort, plunged me into a deep abyss of despair. In a moment of sorrow, I filled a warm bath, clutching a bottle of wine in one hand and a box of opioids in the other. Tears flowed freely for what felt like an eternity. After sipping half the bottle, I resolved to take the tablets, one half at a time, knowing that swallowing them all at once would be an insurmountable feat.

With a handful of tablets poised upon my tongue, I gazed out the window, only to witness Jeep, my sister's spirited dog, triumphantly capturing a rabbit. In a flash, I expelled the tablets, leapt from the bath, donned a robe, and dashed outside to rescue the hapless creature! Clearly, the moment was urgent... I paused, reflecting, "This is not who I am; I possess greater strength than this. This is not the way my sister raised me." Yet again, an animal had come to my rescue. In that pivotal moment, I vowed to transform my life, seeking the divine presence of God and Jesus to guide me forward.

I began my pilgrimage to the church, inviting the divine presence of God into the tapestry of my life. It was during this sacred journey that I encountered my fiancé, a beacon of transformation who illuminated my world anew. Each day, I offer my gratitude to the heavens for his presence in my life. An inexplicable force tugged at my heart and soul, drawing me irresistibly to him. It was as if I were a magnet, yearning to be in his orbit. His very essence ensnared me, but it was his playful banter that truly enchanted me, his dark humour, unparalleled and delightful, resonated deeply. This wit was a balm I had wielded to navigate the shadows of my childhood traumas as I blossomed into adulthood.

I vividly recall the thrill of his first invitation to dinner; I was overjoyed (a dashing man asking me out? Truly, I felt like a delectable ice cream sundae basking in the warm sun). We ventured to a cosy restaurant where we both succumbed to the allure of pizza (my ultimate favourite). His opening question, "Would you like a small one?" sent ripples of laughter through me. Without hesitation, I shot back, "Well, if that's the type of girls you've been with, you have quite the surprise in store." I then turned to the waiter with a sparkle in my eye and declared, "Bring me the largest pizza you have, please!" Thus began our delightful escapades, with our second date transporting us to an all-you-can-eat sushi paradise! I was in bliss, plus, I out-ate him, much to my glee.

Two years into our intertwined journey, a tempest erupted between his mother and stepfather, culminating in her desperate call for rescue. Once more, the dark shadow of alcohol cast its spell, igniting the chaos. This was not an isolated incident; the echoes of past turmoil lingered, with the latest episode nearly thrusting his innocent little brother, just four or five years old, into the grasp of welfare. A concerned social worker warned us that entering the system could shatter his spirit. Turning to my partner, I fervently declared, "Then we shall embrace him under our wings." At that time, my earnings barely grazed R800 a month, a mere trickle for two young souls still navigating the labyrinth of life together.

Stepping into the roles of guardians for the sake of his brother, we found ourselves repeatedly at the police station, caught in the whirlwind of his mom's juvenile disputes. Many nights stretched into the early hours, with us seated in sterile waiting rooms until the clock struck three. It often felt as though we were the caretakers of our own parents amidst this turmoil. With our modest incomes, we ensured that the little one had nourishment, shelter, and a place to learn. We aspired to craft a sanctuary of safety for him, even if it meant sacrificing our own meals to do so. After a span of eight or nine months, his mother was granted the chance to reclaim her little son. Each day, I find inspiration in my partner's strength, as he lights the path for me to embrace my own courage, particularly fortitude in confronting the haunting shadows of my familial past. On the other hand, my partner is blessed with a father that embodies the very essence of wonder, a dad truly remarkable in every sense. His heart shines with the brilliance of gold and expands to encompass the universe. He is the kind of father I longed for in my own childhood dreams. The boundless love he holds for his son is a magnificent tapestry, woven with threads of warmth and affection.

Encountering my partner felt like destiny, yet my father, mother, grandmother, and twin harboured disdain for him. Even now, their feelings remain unchanged. Throughout my life, my partner has been my steadfast pillar of support, teaching me to love in new ways, to embody strength, to embrace tranquillity and to steadfastly chase my dreams of becoming a healer of animals. Despite their relentless efforts to drive him from my life, I reached a turning point where I severed ties with my father entirely. It has been five years since I last saw or spoke to him, and in that silence, I find happiness. I rejoice in the absence of a monster in my life.

My mother, too, has cast shadows over my achievements. When I established my animal healthcare facility, I chose to create it in her garage, a decision she initially embraced. Yet, mere months later, she accused me of robbing her of her home, although it is a spacious five-bedroom dwelling nestled within six acres of land. Each week, she finds new grievances to voice against me. In my quest for understanding, I turned to a therapist, who illuminated the source of her behaviour.

This revelation has prompted deep reflection on my childhood, revealing that this self-centred, drama-loving, and negative individual has always been part of my life. It is clear now why she remained with my father, as her pattern of behaviour aligns with the turmoil I have faced. Everything has fallen into place, shedding light on the complexities of my upbringing.

In the magical month of June 2024, my beloved partner graced me with the most extraordinary proposal of all time! I was swept into a realm of joy, utterly unprepared for such a splendid moment! Among the few who shared in our elation were his father and some cherished friends, along with my sisters and my wonderful brother-in-law. Yet, my mother? She seemed indifferent... His mother mirrored her sentiments. It seemed that the celebration was lost on them. Typically, when a daughter or daughter-in-law becomes engaged, it's the mothers who yearn to orchestrate the festivities. But both of our mothers offered not even a flicker of joy for our union.

What weighs heaviest on my heart is the absence of my father to walk me down the aisle. Yet, why does this sorrow linger? For I am blessed with a remarkable brother-in-law who has been more of a father figure to me than my own. He is the epitome of a loving dad! He has illuminated for me the essence of manhood, fatherhood, and brotherhood. Truly, he stands as my guiding star, alongside my sister, Rex.

Amidst the shadows of trauma, alongside our beloved creatures, I envision a future that aligns with my deepest desires, and I trust that my moment will arrive. My journey with animals, intertwined with the challenges I face with my mother, has illuminated a path towards aiding others like myself through the gentle embrace of these beings. Let the healing powers of animals soothe those enduring hardships. I like to refer to them as "depression companions", be it a cow, a duck, or a dog, each one carries a spark of compassion, and I firmly believe they possess the magic to mend this world, just as they have nurtured my own healing, akin to the support of a service dog.

I yearned for the tender embrace of parental love, only to discover too soon that such affection is not always bestowed freely. My self-reliance is not merely a testament to strength, but a vital skill forged through the fires of disappointment. Though the longing for love from my parents lingers still, I have woven a tapestry of acceptance in the face of its absence.

Reflecting upon the corridors of my past, I feel a deep sense of gratitude for my father. Thank you for embodying a presence that illuminated the paths I wish to avoid in life. Your example has guided me in understanding what to shun when I envision my own family someday. I am grateful for the lessons on the kind of man I do not wish to welcome into my life and for instilling within me a healthy fear of alcoholism. Thank you for revealing that abuse is an unacceptable shadow. Your influence has forged within me a resilient spirit, encouraging me to rise and never surrender.

To my mother, thank you, too. Thank you for illuminating the path of who I should not become and for teaching me that abuse is never acceptable. Thank you for demonstrating the importance of being truly present in the lives of our children and for showing me what boundless love looks like, even in its absence. Thank you for guiding me in how to communicate with our children and, most importantly, for revealing the ways I should avoid. You have forged me into someone better, stronger, and more empowered.

I met with a dear friend's father, a steadfast believer in God and Jesus Christ. Our conversation meandered through the realms of marriage more than family. Yet, unexpectedly, he turned to me and said, "Neevey, you must forgive your parents; otherwise, you will remain shackled by anger and resentment, passing this burden onto your children one day." His words struck a chord, and tears welled in my eyes, as I hadn't anticipated such a profound insight. I then inquired, How does one forgive a monster? How does one find it in their heart to forgive a manipulator who perpetually drags them down? More importantly, how does one forget the shadows of the past? He gently advised that forgiveness is a gift we bestow upon ourselves, not for them, but for our own peace and healing.

From his wisdom, I learned that to forgive is to separate the individual from their transgressions, much like Christ did when He bore our sins. Liking the person is not a requirement. When you choose to forgive and overcome darkness with light, you pave the way for God to be your champion. Forgiveness is the key that unlocks the door to healing. Thus, pray for them, bless them, and release them. In doing so, you dismantle the enemy's hold over your spirit.

I forgive you, Mom and Dad. I bless you in every conceivable way. Thank you for your existence. You are chosen and blameless before God. May the Lord safeguard you, envelop you in peace, and fill your hearts and minds with love. I wish for your prosperity and the blossoming of goodness within you. I understand that you may be navigating life, perhaps recognising your past actions but feeling lost on how to amend them. I, too, have faced regrets, yet they do not define me; the same holds true for you.

I am Neeve, a beacon of strength, power, and love. As the proud founder, CEO, and Veterinary Technician, I established the first primary animal health care sanctuary in South Africa. My journey, woven through the tapestry of a challenging childhood shaped by my parents, ultimately directed my heart and soul toward the noble realm of animals, and I shall steadfastly hold onto my passion for Veterinary Science.

# Women I'm Inspired By

### Granny

My husband's grandmother is a source of inspiration for me in countless beautiful ways. From our first meeting, I was enveloped by her warmth, her quiet strength, and the remarkable grace that surrounds her. There's something uniquely special about her demeanour - with kindness shining in her eyes, wisdom echoing in her words, and a gentle presence that makes everyone feel safe and cherished.

What moves me the most is the life she has led and the way she has confronted every challenge with both courage and dignity. She has weathered many storms, made sacrifices for her family, and loved deeply in a truly exceptional way. Her remarkable ability to stay strong while retaining her softness is a balance I genuinely admire.

Her stories, her values, and the way she unites the family have imparted invaluable lessons about resilience, love, and grace. Being in her presence inspires me to become a better person - more patient, more grateful, and more compassionate. She is not just my husband's grandmother; she embodies the heart of the family, a living testament to strength, love, and legacy.

I feel incredibly fortunate to know her and to learn from her. She inspires me every single day, and I hold immense love and respect for the woman she is and all that she represents.

### Rex

My sister is my idol, as she has been a beacon of light during some of the darkest periods of my life. In our childhood, amidst pain and abuse, she took on the role of my protector, long before we should have had to show such strength. She shielded me in ways that words can scarcely capture - with her bravery, her embrace, and her love. Even as a young girl, she possessed a strength that kept me grounded when everything around us was crumbling.

She instilled hope in me when I was unaware of its existence. She was the one who dried my tears, brought laughter when smiling felt impossible, and reminded me - simply through her presence - that love is genuine and healing can occur. She refused to let our past define us;

instead, she became a living testament to resilience, compassion, and grace.

Today, I see her not merely as my sister but as the person who has moulded the strongest aspects of my character. She is my role model, my sanctuary, and my greatest source of inspiration. I admire her not only for surviving but for choosing love, forgiveness, and to continue shining brightly. She is my idol because, without her, I wouldn't be who I am today.

# Reflections

# Reflections

## Julie Dixon
## Wales

Julie Dixon is an 'Endo Warrior' and advocate for the better treatment and health care of women in Wales, as well as a campaigner for the awareness of fibromyalgia and endometriosis

Julie and her husband have built a wedding business which is based in South Wales over the last 10 years, supplying photobooths, dancefloors and wedding decor, amongst lots of other hire items

Due to medical negligence and ongoing health issues, she has had to take a back seat from the business, but her devoted husband, Adam, runs the day-to-day

Never one to give up, Julie has embarked on an Open University degree course in design and has plans to complete her Master's degree in the future.

She is the fur baby mother of Eddie and Peaches, and loves taking them both to the beach.

# Endo Life

It was the morning of Halloween 2011, and I was checking into Coventry Walsgrave Hospital to have my first-ever baby scan. To say my partner Adam and I were excited to be having our first child was an understatement. We had only been together just over a year at this point, but we were very much in love and knew we both had a place in each other's hearts., I had never met anyone I could have seen myself having kids with before meeting Adam. I came from a broken home. My parents divorced when I was very young, so I wanted to make sure if I was going to start a family, it was going to be with someone I saw my future with I wasn't what you would call a maternal woman, either. I was always working and having fun with friends and socialising. Both Adam and I had careers and loved to travel, so we knew if we were going to have kids, now would have to be the time, as my maternal clock was ticking. I was already thirty-eight.

The thought of pregnancy scared me, as I had a twin brother when I was born. Sadly, he was stillborn. Back in the 1970s, they didn't have scans, so my mother gave birth to me and was sent home. She was later rushed back into the hospital with sepsis, when they discovered she was carrying another baby! My brother was only six months old and had died in her womb. Being pregnant for the first time and remembering the first stories I was told about childbirth must have frightened me more than I knew it had. Growing up in the early eighties in north-west England, if we had a fear of something, we'd say that thing had "done something to my brain", and I am pretty sure, looking back over my life, there was a deep trauma in my mind. I do always wonder what my twin would be like if he were here now, and what having a twin brother would have been like growing up.

My husband Adam is one of five siblings, and all his brothers and sisters have had a minimum of two children each. Adam was the oldest, so it was finally his time to become a father. We were waiting with apprehension in the waiting room for the nurse to call us in. I had never experienced a scan before on my women's bits, so I had no idea what to expect. You could say I was a little nervous. I lay on the table with Adam by my side. As the nurse scanned my tummy, she was asking us questions like when my last period was, etc. We worked out that I was approximately. eight weeks pregnant. She showed us the sac in the womb, but then asked us to wait while she got a doctor to check the scan. The doctor came in, looked at me, and looked back at the scan on the monitor. He scanned me again. I asked, "Is everything ok?" I was getting a little concerned at this point. The doctor said, "I'm very sorry, Julie, but there is no developed heartbeat" I looked at Adam and burst into tears. Our baby had no heartbeat.

The doctor then continued to explain the next steps. I could either take a pill and it would induce a miscarriage, or I could wait for the baby "to come away naturally." I couldn't hold back my tears. Adam just looked devastated. The doctors and nurses were genuinely nice, but as they see this all the time and deal with baby loss daily, they were a little matter-of-fact for my liking. I felt like I had to quickly make a choice in amongst my confusion, grief, and pain. I opted for the pill that would induce the miscarriage. I remember the nurse saying at this point, "It's very common that one in three women experience miscarriage." I found it shocking as I didn't know any woman who had gone through this. For some reason, when women talk about their first scans, it's full of joy and printed photos or 3D videos. I was given two pills. One was taken there and then, and then I was told to go home and take the other pill twelve hours later. I was told I would need to go back to get re-scanned in a week to make sure the foetus had "come away."

As we left the ward and entered the corridor, I collapsed on the floor in tears. I was utterly heartbroken. Our dreams of being a family had gone. That evening, I felt numb. Adam was trying his best to stay strong, but I could tell he was struggling. Then the contractions started; yes, contractions! I wasn't told this would happen at the hospital. Nothing was explained in detail to either me or Adam, so there was no reason why this happened. It's just one of those things that happen, and as women, we have to accept it. At this time, we had to go through three miscarriages before any investigations were done into what was causing them. Going through a miscarriage once was bad enough, but multiple times? The contractions were light twinges in my tummy. There was odd flicker of pain every now and then throughout the evening. The next morning, I went to the toilet... and there it was, our baby, our dream. The sack had come away. I returned to the hospital a week later for another scan and some blood tests. The doctors confirmed the miscarriage, and I was told I had an RH-negative blood type. This meant I had to have an injection to prevent further complications in future pregnancies. If a mother is RH-negative, her immune system can attack the baby's red blood cells and cause something called 'Blue Baby;' basically, my blood type could cause my body to reject the child. My own blood was fighting my desire to have a baby. I felt completely numb and lost. My hormones were all over the place, and I couldn't stop crying. I had experienced a lot of loss in my life up to this point. I'd lost a lot of people I loved, and losing this baby just felt like the final straw, the icing on the cake. I found it awful how cruel people could be in the next few months. I was told "just to move on," "try again," "put it behind you." I was told to "snap out of it," "move forward," "forget it" and "this happens all the time!" Suggestions in the form of questions, such as "what about fostering? or adopting?" are especially hurtful. It was women who were saying the above, and they all had their own children. Whether they had gone through miscarriage themselves, who knows, but no one talks about the dark side of pregnancy. All we hear are the success stories. No one wants to talk about the heartbreak; maybe if someone had talked to me about it, I would have been aware that one in three pregnancies end in miscarriage. I would have been prepared before I went into the scan room that the baby might not have a heartbeat.

After this ordeal, I decided to get the contraceptive implant put into my arm. I needed some time to heal before Adam and I tried again. I wasn't equipped to deal with it again. Job prospects in Coventry at the time were not great. I was from London and had moved to Coventry to live with Adam. We used to take weekend trips to Cardiff to visit an old school friend of Adam's, and we discovered we loved Cardiff and South Wales. So, we decided to relocate and start afresh.

A few years passed and myself and Adam hit the big forty, and we felt settled. We had a nice home and jobs, so we decided to try for another baby. I felt stronger, but there was always this nagging feeling in the back of my mind that something was wrong with me. It was hard to know whether the nagging feeling was anxiety or an actual thing. I had to give it another go. Not just for me, but for Adam, too. He wanted to be a dad, and I know his family would have loved another baby in the family. And, of course, I wanted to have a child with the man I loved. The implant was removed, and we set out to try again for another baby. That's when all hell broke loose. Not long after the implant was removed, I started to experience very heavy periods and crushing pain. This would last for around two weeks. The pain felt like I was being stabbed in my ovaries, and the blood loss was so heavy I couldn't leave the house. Luckily, I had a job working from home.

I decided to see my GP as something didn't feel right; I didn't remember my periods being this bad. I'd had the implant in my arm for years. I saw a male GP and I explained my symptoms. The intense pelvic pain, needing to go to the loo all the time, heavy bleeding, large clots of blood that were the size of my palm, and an excruciating pain when I went for a number two, like someone had shoved a knife up my backside. I had no energy and had terrible fatigue. I felt like I had barbed wire wrapped around my ovaries. The doctor said, "I am going to take some bloods, one of which being a CA 125 as this helps diagnose ovarian cancer". My anxiety was through the roof at this point. I was thinking the worst, but when you're bleeding as heavily as I was, and the pain was so intense it was hard to feel any other way. The GP said, "It is likely your weight" Yes, my weight! I was like, "Are you kidding me? How are these symptoms anything to do with my weight?" Had he listened to anything I had said? I was confused. I was a little curvy, yes, but didn't feel that overweight, He then said, it could be IBS." I felt like he hadn't listened to a word I had said. I left the doctor's office in tears. The blood tests came back "fine apart from a little anaemia", which was likely to be the fact that I was losing lots of blood monthly.

A friend of mine from Coventry, Lucy, had issues with her periods, so I decided to reach out to her. I explained my symptoms to her, and she said, "Oh my gosh, Julie, it really does sound like endometriosis." She also said, "if a period disrupts your life this badly something isn't right. A period shouldn't leave you in crippling pain!" "What's Endometriosis?" I asked. I'd never heard of it. I knew she had a few issues every month, but we never really discussed them. This is a big part of the problem; women don't really discuss periods. It's the unsaid, something we don't talk about on a night out over dinner. My friend Lucy encouraged me to go to another GP and ask for a referral to a gynaecologist, one who specialises in Endometriosis. Off I went again to the GP, and this time I saw a female GP. After I had explained everything, she finally referred me to a gynaecologist at the hospital.

There was a long wait to see someone, so another year passed by. This time, our dream of having a family seemed like a very distant one. I was in such a physical mess that I couldn't even go through the process of trying to make a baby. I was bleeding for two weeks every month, and sex was painful. I felt like I was bleeding to death most days. Using normal sanitary towels was useless. I had to get what I called "nana pads" the large pads older ladies wear for urine leakage. These pads were changed hourly, even though they were super absorbent. I would stand up and feel blood running down my leg. I'd have to run to the toilet, and you can see how leaving the house was challenging. I would go for a poo, and it would feel like my insides were being ripped out. The pain would make me sweat and feel really sick. Just the simple task of having a poo would feel like what friends would say labour feels like. I had to breathe like a pregnant woman in labour. Seeing that there was blood in my stools, my mind went somewhere else: "Oh no! Maybe it was my bowels!" Knowing what blood in the poo meant, I was so frightened. Again, I went back to the GP. I was referred for a colonoscopy. Meanwhile, I was still waiting to see a gynaecologist. Nothing was reported as abnormal from the colonoscopy. I had X-rays and scans of my bowel, bladder, all my women's parts, but nothing. Medically, there nothing was wrong with me. The GP tried to put me back on the pill, but it didn't stop the pain or the bleeding. I was also given a tablet that stops internal bleeding in the body, but this didn't work either.

I was desperate to find out what was going on. I had some serious life-altering symptoms, but no one could find out what was happening. Discovering an endometriosis group on Facebook, I tried to get answers to what was happening to me, even though at this point, I didn't have a diagnosis. From talking with the other women, I was convinced I had Endo- the name those of us who live with it choose to call it. Talking with these other women and getting advice from them was my only source of information and real support. My days and nights were spent on the sofa with an electric heat pad on my tummy. I used to have it so hot it would leave red burn marks on my body, but the heat helped the pain. I tried various painkillers, and the GP started me on Paracetamol. This did nothing for the pain, as you would expect. After numerus trips back and forth to the GP, I was given various medications - none of which helped the pain. I was given one fo the strongest painkillers available in the end, and that only took the edge off the pain slightly.
I was also told to try a TENS machine, which pregnant ladies use at the onset of labour. It helped the pain slightly as it's a nerve stimulation device that pulses electrical currents into the muscles to help them relax. My tummy looked like I was nine months pregnant. I was getting contraction pains and felt like I wanted to push something out. It felt very similar to the miscarriage, and this was my monthly reminder of what was to come. I would push and huge clots would come out. It honestly made me feel sick. This was a cruel illness to experience. The pain every month was like labour, but with no baby bliss at the end of the pain, just torture.

My first gyno appointment came a year and a half later. I was lucky enough to be living in Cardiff, as the team at the hospital I'd been referred to was an Endometriosis specialist. This team of people were the only Endo specialists in South Wales, which is crazy as one in ten women suffer from the illness. One team of people to look after all these women!? Something had to be done about this, and I knew I wanted to help. There was no test for Endometriosis, and the only formal way to diagnose it is to undergo a laparoscopy, where doctors insert a camera into the tummy to check for something called Endo Lesions. After explaining all my symptoms to the specialist, he agreed it certainly sounded like Endo. Finally! Someone who was listening and understood what I was going through - well, as much as a man can understand

Endo! I'd been told it was my weight, IBS, Crohn's Disease, Diverticulitis, Cancer and even a burst appendix. The laparoscopy was booked for six months, which sounds like a long time, but this was quick. According to the Endometriosis website[1] at the time of going to press with this book, it takes a woman seven and a half years to be diagnosed with Endometriosis.

The laparoscopy surgery day came, and thankfully, it was a day surgery. Whilst waiting for the surgery, my thoughts ran away with themselves. What if they don't find Endo? Then what? What if it's all in my head? Going through surgery seemed like an extreme way to get a diagnosis, but it was the only way I could get answers. I really didn't want to feel like all this surgery was for nothing, especially if there was no Endo. Then what? I was given a general anaesthetic, and a few hours later, I came around. I woke up in the recovery room to a nurse trying to wake me up. The first words I said were, "Did they find endometriosis?" "YES," she said. They found a lot of Endo legions. The doctor will come round later and have a chat with you." The relief I felt was overwhelming. I cried with relief. I wanted to get up out of bed there and then and race to the original GP who'd told me it was my weight and tell him he was wrong! Completely wrong! I had endometriosis; I wasn't happy that I had this illness. Far from it, but I was happy I had finally gotten answers. And like many women, I had to fight to get these answers. The diagnosis, the Endo specialist told me later that evening, was that he'd found Endo on my pelvic wall, bladder, pouch of Douglas[2], on both ovaries, and bowel - and fallopian tubes! He had also taken a sample of my uterus, as I had what is called a "bulky uterus." He said, "It's likely to be caused by Adenomyosis. This is known as Endo's big sister." Due to the amount of Endo within my body, I would need another surgery to remove it all. I was advised by him that this would help with the pain and help with fertility. I was sent home that evening feeling relieved - and with so many questions. The main one being "what future fertility would look like?" I was told I would be put on the waiting list for another surgery and would receive a letter in the post.

My gynaecologist checked in with me a few weeks afterwards and confirmed the sample of my uterus was Adenomyosis. "Ok... so what does this mean?" I asked. He explained he could take out the

Endo, but unfortunately, to remove the Adenomyosis, it would require a full hysterectomy; I wasn't ready for this news, and certainly not ready for a hysterectomy! I was still in my early forties! And I hadn't had children! After some quick thinking, I agreed with the gyno that we would remove the endometriosis first, just to see if it would help my fertility. I had to wait a further year for my next laparoscopy to remove the Endometriosis. At this point, I was too frightened for Adam and me to try for a baby, as I knew I had all these issues and the last thing I wanted for me and Adam was another miscarriage. I was also forty-two at this point, so my age also made it a high-risk pregnancy. Adam felt helpless seeing me in so much pain. The last thing on his mind was having a baby. He just wanted his wife to have a pain-free life. The feelings of uselessness swept over me. All our friends had children. Why couldn't I do this for Adam? I honestly felt like a terrible wife. Adam said he didn't marry me to produce his child; he married me because he loved me and wanted to spend his life with me. If we had kids, it would be a bonus. I could see how much the physical pain I had upset him, as there wasn't anything he could do about it.

Life was on hold until I could get the Endo removed and hopefully feel fitter and, in less pain. I was in a state of limbo, just waiting for surgery and letters from the hospital. There was nothing more I could do, but every day that passed, my maternal clock was ticking away. Booked in for my second surgery and nil my mouth again, I was relieved it was a day surgery. The specialist explained they would go in and remove the Endometriosis, some of which were close to organs like my bowel and bladder. There is a risk of damage during the surgery and a general anaesthetic, but at this point, I was ready to take that risk. The doctors pumped me full of gas as they do for a laparoscopy, and a few hours later, the Endo was removed. This wasn't a permanent fix, as Endo can grow back, and there is always a risk that it will never completely go away. With the Adenomyosis to contend with at this point, we didn't know what was really causing the pain and bleeding. Both Adam and I had reached the point of relief that the Endo had been removed.

After the surgery, the specialist said a lot of the Endo legions they'd removed were old legions, and it was likely they had been in there for some years. As I was on the pill for most of my twenties and thirties, I never realised I had these issues. Not realising all those years that something was wrong, because I was on the pill, hit me hard. Had I known years ago that something could have been done before it got as bad as it had, it would have meant I might have had a chance of being a mother, but the pill just covered up the symptoms. And if this was the case for me, how many other women were living this truth? It really annoys me when I hear of young women going to the GP with heavy periods and pain, and instead of doctors investigating the issue. Young girls and women are simply given the pill during which time Endometriosis is growing on their organs like Japanese knotweed, causing severe and irreparable damage - damage that can affect their fertility. Hearing this news, I knew something had to change. After the surgery, Adam and I decided to try for a baby. Nothing was really happening. Sex was still painful, and the daily pain remained. Life didn't change much. Yes, the Endometriosis they'd removed was adding to the pain I was feeling before surgery, but it wasn't that; the main issue was the Adenomyosis. As my uterus was so big and bulky, it was pushing on my bowel, which caused the pain I felt when pooing. I was feeling it was pressing on my bladder, hence why I felt like I needed to go to the loo constantly. Due to the size of my uterus, I looked pregnant all the time. All the symptoms I had been suffering from were starting to make sense.

The realisation of a hysterectomy was starting to sink in, and with it followed depression. I was never going to be pain-free until I had my uterus and ovaries removed. I knew I couldn't continue the way I was, so a choice was going to have to be made. Adam and I agreed to go and see my gyno to discuss what my current fertility situation was like. We wanted to know what my actual chances of having a child were going to be, we would get IVF on the NHS and would it even help? The meeting with the gyno didn't go well. He said, looking at the current situation, there was about a ten per cent chance of falling pregnant, with a high risk of miscarriage. "What about IVF?" I asked. He responded with, "I'll email the IVF team and see if they will see you." I was shocked! "What do you mean, 'If they will see me!? Surely someone like me should be top of the list for IVF because of my age and problems!" We needed the help to get pregnant, and there had already been enough delays and errors made by doctors within the NHS. The IVF team promptly replied to the email with a refusal to see me. I wasn't even offered a meeting or a chat. It was firm no; "No point. It won't work," they said. That was it. The dream of having a baby gone. Unless there was some miraculous intervention where I would fall pregnant and have a full-term, amazing pregnancy - and my name is Julie, not Mary, so the chances of that were slim. I felt so angry. Confused, too. Surely that's what IVF teams do! Surely, they help women like me. With no chances of even getting an appointment on the NHS, and no funds to allow us to go private, I had to come to terms with not having my own child with the man I loved. With feelings of bitterness and depression setting in, I would avoid friends with children as I couldn't bear to be around them. I would avoid going to Adam's family parties as I knew all his brothers and sisters would be there with their kids. Hiding away from the world became my norm, and home became both my sanctuary and my self-imposed isolation. With more follow-up appointments at the gyno, I waited, and avoided, for a long time, proceeding with further treatment. I knew the next stage was the hysterectomy - and I was still waiting for my miraculous baby. Another two years passed with no sign of me conceiving. Meanwhile, I was still bleeding to death every month, looking nine months pregnant and in agonising pain.

At a follow up appointment with my gyno to discuss options I was given the choices of going back on the pill or having the coil fitted. I had tried both and they didn't work. There was a third option, injections which medically induced menopause. Medically induced menopause with injections means they put the body into temporary menopause. I wasn't ready for a hysterectomy, and I certainly wasn't ready for the menopause! But the only other option was a full hysterectomy. The injection is a very potent drug. It's also used as a cancer drug for men with prostate cancer and can cause bone thinning, menopause symptoms, allergic reactions, and guess what! Vaginal bleeding! Great! Just what I needed! More vaginal bleeding with a side helping of lots of other side effects - way too many to list! If it worked, I was advised, "it would stop your periods and pain for six months and hopefully, give you an idea what menopause will be like." WOW. A taster of the menopause. Just what every woman has on her bucket list! The best part? This 'taster' would only be temporary. With lots of deliberation and discussions, I decided to avoid the hysterectomy and go with the injection. I had to do something. I was now badly anaemic and bleeding to death every month. My ovaries were trying to kill me. After the injection, I headed home.

That night, whilst in the bath, I sat there and burst into uncontrollable crying. I couldn't see through the tears. I felt like I couldn't breathe. Adam rushed upstairs, asking what was wrong. I said, "I have no idea. I just can't stop crying." That night, my back felt like it was on fire, and I had to ask Adam to fetch freezing cold towels to cool me down. What was happening? Was this a side effect of the Prostrap injection? Were these menopause symptoms already?

With hives appearing on my tummy, my back and then my arms and legs, I knew something was terribly wrong. Hives were everywhere, and I felt like I was on fire, and the itchy feeling was intense. Once again, I returned to the GP who gave me antihistamines, which didn't work in the slightest. The hives got worse, and I ended up in A&E. The next day, I was given steroid injections and told I'd had an allergic reaction to the another kind of injection. No shit! I was in a real mess, and my skin was really sore. Could things get any worse? Thank God the treatment from A&E worked, and the hives finally calmed down after a week or so. There was some good news, though: my periods had stopped! And I wasn't bleeding anymore for any other reason. The injections had done their job, in that respect, but I knew I couldn't have any more injections due to the allergic reaction I'd had. With nerve damage in my pelvis from the Endo removal, moving around was painful. I was still spending time with my heat pad, and the pain in my tummy was getting better. With this new awareness, the answer I needed was staring me in the face: I had to have a hysterectomy to make this permanent. A full hysterectomy was a scary choice, but what other choice did I have? Due to medical negligence and being fobbed off, I had been robbed of my choice. I wanted my life back. I wanted to live a pain-free life. I didn't want Adam to see me in pain all the time when there was nothing he could do about it. Then COVID hit, and with all the hospitals on standby for the rush of COVID cases, we were told there were to be no non-emergency operations happening. Was what I was going through, and had been through, not making me an emergency case? Obviously not!

Two years passed before things at the hospital even began to return to anywhere near normal. I'd been on the waiting list for a hysterectomy for three years by this point, and there was a huge backlog of women in the area waiting for gynaecological operations. I knew the hysterectomy was not going to happen any time soon. Things got worse. The pain of going to the toilet was excruciating. My uterus was so enlarged by this point that it was pushing on my bowel and other organs. My spine and pelvis were in bits, meaning I couldn't hardly walk. I would go for a poo and scream the house down; It felt like I was being stabbed with a thousand knives. The pain took my breath away, and I would collapse with exhaustion on the bathroom floor. With no social life and the inability to work due to fatigue and pain, depression was sinking in big time. Not only did I have to face the fact that I couldn't have kids, but physical intimacy and sex was also non-existent because it hurt too much. My life became a mix of watching a lot of Netflix and covering myself with heated blankets with painkillers to treat the pain. Painkillers had become a daily staple in my life. I had been on a particular painkiller for most of this time and was then moved onto another one, as the first one wasn't touching the pain anymore. I was worried about opioid addiction, especially as I had been taking these tablets for more than five years. With advice from the doctors telling me that even when I come off them, if ever I did, then I would have to gradually taper the dose. The doctor even mentioned the possibility of having to take methadone to get me off the opioids! Great! Like I didn't have enough issues to deal with, I now had the joys of looking forward to withdrawal from opioids! Not taking them wasn't an option. I couldn't live without them. The pain was too intense, and they were the only medication that even slightly helped reduce the pain.

Meeting with my friend Lucy for coffee, another Endo sufferer, was always a welcome release. She was a wonderful lady who had supported me throughout this journey. Lucy never minced her words, and as an advocate for women's rights and health care, she knew how to get heard. She'd had her own struggles with endometriosis, and she explained, "We have to shout louder to get the help we need." She begged me to appeal against the IVF refusal to treat me, but by this time, I was exhausted from the whole thing.

I was now mid-forties, and I was too tired to fight. I just wanted my life back. Explaining to Lucy that I'd waited years for the hysterectomy, she said, "You must complain to PALs - the hospital liaison service!" Lucy helped me to understand just how many women were waiting for these operations, and sitting back and waiting for the letter wasn't going to work. I *must* shout louder. It's the only way. "The more your voice is heard, the quicker the treatment will come."

Knowing then what I know now, I may have fought harder to get IVF treatments, but with the blood loss, the pain, the mental and emotional exhaustion, I had hardly anything left in me to get up in the day, let alone fight the system. But she was right, and I knew it. Unless I was on the phone with the hospital, standing my ground, nothing was going to get done quickly - or at all. It wasn't the hospital's fault in many respects, especially as they had such a backlog. I also knew how hard the Endo nurses and doctors worked and didn't want to come across as though I was ungrateful for their support. But I had to do something. I contacted PALs (Patient Advice and Liaison Service)[3] at the hospital, the official complaints service, and they agreed I was waiting way too long for the hysterectomy and said, "Leave it with us." I had a call from the hospital management, a lovely lady, and she explained. "I am going to action your operation as soon as possible and speak to the surgical team. Will you be available at any time for an operation?" Of course, I said, "Yes!" Within two weeks, I was contacted by the hospital manager and booked for my hysterectomy on the 19th of December. I was in shock, it was happening in two weeks - and it was Christmas- but I couldn't say no after the kick-off I'd made, and what the manager of the hospital had done. She said she would get it sorted for me, and she did. And so, I was booked in for my uterus eviction. The lead-up to the removal day was an emotional roller-coaster. It was bittersweet as I wanted a family so badly, but I also wanted to live a normal, pain-free life without bleeding to death every month. Adam had also reached the point where he wanted me to have the hysterectomy. He knew it was the only other option; enough was enough.

The day of surgery, I hadn't slept. I was worried about the procedure as well as the aftermath. I checked into Cardiff hospital, gowned myself up, and got ready for my full hysterectomy to remove the Adenomyosis. As I lay there, in tears, waiting to be sent down for surgery, I called

Adam. A last-minute freak-out was well underway, as I didn't want to go ahead with it. I knew it was so final. Once they'd removed everything, they couldn't exactly put it all back again. Adam calmed me down between my tears and declarations that "I want to get dressed and come home" and "But we wanted to have a family." Adam reassured me he wasn't worried any more about kids. He knew there was no hope. And all that mattered to him was having a healthier wife, one who was pain-free and happy. He reminded me, "I didn't marry you for you to produce my babies. I married you because I love you and want to spend the rest of my life with you." After his reassurance, not only did I calm down and decide to stay put, but I felt genuinely loved for me. My surgeon explained how he would "remove the ovaries, fallopian tubes, cervix and uterus." So, all my womanly bits and bobs. The operation went well. I woke up in the recovery room, and it was done by keyhole surgery. I spent that night in the hospital. I remember feeling very empty not only emotionally, but physically. My '9-month pregnant belly' I'd been carrying around my deformed uterus in had gone, my tummy felt empty, I felt empty.

I spent that night feeling lost and couldn't wait to get home to Adam - and my beloved dog Peaches. The next day, I was grateful to be going home. Packed off with painkillers, I was told to speak to my GP about HRT and what to expect during the menopause. Being told I would need to take HRT was another smack in the face. Having the hysterectomy meant I would go into what they call 'surgical menopause.' Yes, menopause. I was only mid-forties! No one had really discussed menopause with me, not even my own mother. I thought it would be a few hot sweats, nothing to stress about - I had been through a lot worse leading up to the operation, so I was sure I could handle a few hot flushes. Oh, how so little did I know!

It was now a few days before Christmas, and I was so pleased Adam was home to take care of me. I had the next few months to "rest up." Christmas Eve was awful. I remember crying my eyes out just looking at my Facebook feed. Everywhere I looked, I saw pictures of my friends and family with their children. On Christmas Day, I stayed away from Facebook. Seeing photos of all the happy families was more than I could take. It was painful emotionally, especially as Christmas is, in my opinion, the worst time to have a hysterectomy, especially for someone who can't have children. Christmas is *all about* the kids, and I wouldn't have that excitement with my children. I felt like everyone else had this experience that I would never have - because of my stupid uterus. There's this feeling like you have missed out on a huge part of being a woman. It makes you question if you are even really a woman if you do not have a uterus.

I believed in God, but I wouldn't say I am the best Christian in the world. Going to church every week wasn't something I did, but I believed, and I prayed; God knows I prayed! I knew He was in control of my life during these last few years, but my faith felt shattered. I believed children were a gift from God, so why wasn't I blessed with this gift? Why did He not want me to have children?

Seeing stories on the news of people mistreating their kids made me so angry. How were these people able to have kids? If kids were a gift from God, why did He give them to these abusers, but not someone like me who would love and treasure them? I started to feel very bitter in my faith and my beliefs.

My recovery physically went well after the operation, but inside, I was broken. I didn't feel like a woman anymore. I felt empty inside. I had no career and no hopes of having a family. No hopes of being a mum. With no direction, the only thing I knew was I had a husband who loved me, and for that I was grateful. I was grateful to Adam every day he looked after me, picked me up off the floor when I was in tears, and I was grateful he supported me through this emotionally unstable time. Isolation kicked in as I avoided all my friends with children as much as possible because it was just too painful.

With my hormones on the rampage, they needed fixing. I was now in the menopause. There was no perimenopause as would naturally happen. There were no slow signs or an easing in gently. Oh, no. I woke up and was in full-blown menopause. I was given anti-depressants and HRT from the GP, as well as an oestrogen gel I rub on the inside top of my leg every night. The next few years was all about getting my hormone levels right and starting the road to recovery, mentally, emotionally, physically, socially, and spiritually.

On this road of getting my hormones right, I'm learning the menopause isn't just the hot sweats people talk about. It is insomnia, muscle pain all over the body, depression, and anxiety. Emotions are all over the place. I gain weight just thinking about food. Then there is the low self-esteem, brain fog, memory loss, hair thinning, fatigue, itchy skin, gut and digestion issues, restless legs, reduced sex drive, joint aches and much more. The list is endless. Great. Thanks, God!

I asked myself why all wasn't this explained to me in detail by the hospital, but it's not after the hysterectomy is completed that you must speak to your GP to organise your HRT. Why are women not given full informed consent? There is no follow-up after the hysterectomy or menopause after care, so I haven't been back to the hospital since the operation. I really feel there should be more aftercare support for women who are plunged into surgical menopause.

My friend Lucy, my "speak as loud as you can friend", decided to get me involved with the yearly Endometriosis awareness march. A protest through Cardiff that takes place once a year as a group of Endo warriors raise awareness, marching through the city centre. Awareness of the illness and the length of time it takes for diagnosis are the key issues that need to be raised. Women need to know about this, as do our husbands, fathers, employers, and the wider community.

I've met some wonderful women on the Endo march team, which consists of a group of women who've had years of experience with Endometriosis; most of who have been suffering since being a teenager. Some have had multiple surgeries to remove their Endo, and some are still suffering. Some women have ended up with colostomy bags after losing use of their bowels due to Endometriosis. Some women have had such bad nerve damage that they can't walk and have ended up in wheelchairs. Others have suffered multiple miscarriages, and this is why we are called "Endo Warriors" - We are literally fighting battles against our own bodies. It is nice to be part of an organisation of like-minded people, and I have made good friends from being part of the Endo march Wales. Meeting women who all had similar stories as mine was a Godsend. I also go to virtual meetings with different surgeons from across the country and different local MPs. Being part of the Endometriosis Awareness Team has given me purpose, and we aim to improve the funding for Endo treatments in Wales. We work closely with FTWW (Future Treatment for Women in Wales).

In a virtual meeting with a representative from Endometriosis UK, a Welsh Endometriosis surgeon from north Wales, and a local MP, questions were being allowed from the virtual online audience. The MP read out my question detailing what had happened to me with the IVF team refusing me an appointment and refusing to see me.

The professional panel said I should have been offered an appointment and was shocked I hadn't been able to at least speak with the IVF team to discuss my options. They confirmed that the IVF team are there to help women who struggle to get pregnant, and that I should have been on top of the list for IVF and should have been given an appointment. At this point, I was so angry. I felt let down and knew I should have shouted louder for treatment. I shouldn't have just taken "no" for an answer. After this enlightenment, I sent an email of complaint to the hospital and the IVF team. The reply from the hospital stated that PALs don't deal with IVF complaints, so I had to contact the IVF team directly. So, I did, and I had no reply from the IVF team. No response whatsoever. This is the reason why I have agreed to take part in this book. I want to tell women to never give up, and if you're struggling like I was, shout louder for the treatments you deserve and are entitled to.

I have made peace with myself now, even though I was let down. I understand that life has a different path for me, and having children isn't one of them, for now. In the future, we may look into fostering. But for now, I have two lovely dogs, Eddie and Peaches, and I have a wonderful husband. I thank God every day for them. As for my faith, I have made peace with that, too. I understood that God doesn't always give us what we want; He has his plan for us and will only give us what we can handle. If I had fallen pregnant again, I may have ended up with a stillborn baby or had multiple miscarriages; all of which were possible. That would have meant more heartache, something that I knew would have been too much for me to deal with. I was very fragile emotionally. Maybe the lord saw that being pregnant wouldn't have ended well for me and would have broken me even more than I already was. It was for that reason I understood why this happened as it did. I am so grateful to the Endo team in Cardiff for how they treated me under the stretched budgets from the Welsh government. They do their best.

At the time of writing, I'm still trying to get my hormones at the right levels. Having been diagnosed with Fibromyalgia, a condition that is regularly diagnosed alongside Endometriosis, I have nerve damage in my pelvis. Thankfully, there is no sign of Endometriosis returning, because yes, it can return even though I don't have ovaries. It can grow on other organs like the bladder and bowel, but thankfully, there is no sign of a return. I will always live with Endo, and the hysterectomy wasn't a cure for Endometriosis, but it removed the Adenomyosis.

I will continue advocating for Endo and campaigning for better treatment for women. I have seen the heartbreak firsthand and what the illness can do to women. Not just the women, but all the good men out there supporting them. It's not just the women's health that is destroyed. It is families, relationships and it takes a tough couple to go through it. It's not nice seeing your partner in pain every day, and there isn't anything they can do about it. I now fill my life with other joys, like spending time with my amazing dogs. They are my kids. We have our holidays, and Adam and I enjoy life as a married couple. We are closer than ever, and Adam is truly my best friend. I do worry about what will happen when I'm old. My friends have their children to help look after them. I won't have that. But one thing I do know I have is an amazing husband. I dedicate this to him because without him and his support, I would have struggled to carry on.

*If any women are reading this, and your period disrupts your life, if normal Paracetamol doesn't take away pain, and if it affects your enjoyment of life, it's not normal. You must see a GP and go to a gynaecologist.*

Globally, it is estimated that around 190 million women suffer from endometriosis. Those are the ones we know about. And in the UK, one in ten women are diagnosed with Endo. It's as common as diabetes and asthma. Young people need to be educated about Endo in schools and need to learn from a young age what a "normal period" is. Young women shouldn't just be put on a pill if they have heavy periods. An investigation into why they are heavy needs to happen.

*Women shouldn't have to go through three miscarriages before investigations are looked into.*

The future of women's health in Wales is looking brighter with the help of FTWW and Endometriosis UK. Different charities are working with schools and young people to educate them, but there is certainly more work to be done. The UK government need to invest more in women's health. and start listening to the women who are fighting to be heard. Women also need to discuss reproductive health more with each other. Period talk wasn't something I discussed before my Endo diagnosis. Maybe if we discussed these things more, it wouldn't be taboo. Periods are a natural occurrence. All women have periods, baby loss and menopause. It's happening to all women all over the world every day, and the more we speak about it, the more women that can be helped and supported.

# Reflections

# Reflections

## Amanda Denham
## United States

Amanda Denham is an artist, illustrator and author born in Alabama. As a teenager, young adult books and comics helped her through challenging times, which inspired her to write stories highlighting mental health awareness for the youth. Her illustrations have been featured in her own novels and other authors' books, and she freelances as an illustrator for books, magazines, and other media productions.

Her artwork fits well in children's story books, young adult novels, cartoons and moving pictures for any tale that aims to show impactful, creative views of mental health struggles.

In the meantime, she also enjoys reading, listening to true crime podcasts, playing with her pet rabbits, and spending time with the people she loves.

Instagram @a.denham
Https://facebook.com/a.denhamcreations

# Art Therapy

I'm surprised that I made it through school with decent grades, because when I flipped through old notebooks, all I saw were doodles littering the pages. Even as far back as five years old, I remember getting done with a task as fast as possible so I could turn the sheet over and draw on the blank side. It never felt like a decision, but instead a compulsion. Almost like art grabbed me and didn't let go before I even knew what it really was. My favourites seemed to be Simba from The Lion King, or my rendition of a person at the time, which consisted of an obviously true-to-life triangle body and stick legs. Little "masterpieces" of the young mind.

As I grew, my influences changed. Disney was a huge one for a while, along with young adult novels. My biggest art influence came when I was introduced to manga, which are Japanese comics. The style was delicate and colourful, full of flowing lines and expressive eyes. Women had become my main subject for a long time, and these influences only enhanced my love for drawing them. I was enamoured with the stories of girls who looked unassuming on the outside but showed undeniable courage when their situations got tough. They were often surrounded by loyal friends, a chosen family who helped keep them motivated when they felt down. It was the perfect formula for my teenage mind: love, beauty, strength, and never giving in to the negative forces that life has dealt me.

A dream began to form; I wanted to tell stories, too. I drew my characters obsessively with their plot points in mind. This practice is still how most of my book ideas come to fruition: an image forms in my head from some sort of inspiration, and I mull over the plot points as I sketch out the characters. Many things can be lost when adulthood is reached, but I'm glad this has stayed with me. The vibrant visuals give me a head start on understanding the aesthetic of the book I want to write. Hopefully, I've only gotten better since I was a teenager, since I actually write my stories now, versus just drawing about them.

My family was usually supportive of my art. They were made up of my parents, my older sister, and my younger brother. Before you ask, yes, I suffer *greatly* from Middle Child Syndrome.

According to my mother, my younger years were spent following my big sister around, as did my brother. We were a tight-knit group of siblings for a while, often playing with our Power Rangers toys or acting out Disney movies together. My parents worked varying shifts so that we wouldn't have to go to daycare. While that is admirable, I think it's also the reason why we really didn't have any friends until our middle school years. We had each other then, and we didn't know anything other than that. Looking back on it, we really were in an immediate family bubble. We didn't have much interaction with my parents' siblings, and it became less and less as we aged. Sadly, all of our grandparents had passed away by the time we were born, except my mother's mom. She developed Alzheimer's when I turned seven or eight, so she isn't the real "her" in the memories I do have.

Thankfully, being a child meant that I was happy with the way things were for a long time. You only know as much as you've seen and what you're taught. My parents worked extremely hard to provide for us at the expense of a social life. I remember my mom having a couple of friends she interacted with, none that I can think of for my dad. It makes me sad for them, almost like they gave up everything once we were born. I've heard it was common to do so back then in the eighties - focus only on your kids, everything else fell to the wayside. I hope nowadays there is more balance in people's lives. Everyone deserves friends, people they can rely on when life gets too rough.

We all loved each other, of course, but we girls especially bonded. My mom was the one I went to for anything emotional. She'd listen patiently to our teenage gossip, give advice about boys, and have fun with us along the way. Some of my favourite younger memories are when we'd gather together on Tuesday or Thursday nights to catch the newest episodes of "Smallville" or "Friends." My mom didn't even mind if my friends or boyfriend at the time joined. She was always supportive of my art, always saying I was talented. Having a person you admire and trust giving you that kind of encouragement. It's invaluable to an adolescent mind. I had nowhere else to pull the confidence from. If she believed in me, then maybe those dreams could become reality.

Unfortunately, those dreams went nowhere for quite a while.

My parents fought often, especially in my teenage years. To be honest, I barely remember what a lot of the arguments were about. I'd often leave the house or try to do something to distract myself if I heard them. I justified it in my mind as something that married adults did sometimes. While it was rough to experience, I felt it was normal. Other friends my age had confided in me about parental troubles, so it seemed to line up that this was just a thing that happened. And if something was normal, then surely things would be okay eventually.

What I didn't expect was for my parents to break up the way they did. When I was sixteen, my father caught my mom in some big lies and immediately declared that he was kicking her out of the house. At first, I was sceptical. I didn't trust him as much as my mom. However, direct evidence doesn't lie, and soon I had to accept that my mom had not only lied to him, but to all of us. Memories flooded back of times when she'd ask me not to tell him certain things, and again, I took that as normal. Dad was often a very jovial man, but sometimes he seemed to get upset quickly and randomly about small things. I always thought it was the same as when she'd cover for me if I went to hang out with my boyfriend; we had each other's backs. No use getting him upset if he didn't have to know.

Now, I wonder how much was being hidden that even I wasn't privy to. I was too in the dark and way too young to make my own assumptions. My biggest concerns at sixteen were school and my social life. I didn't understand the intricacies of a twenty-year marriage and the betrayal of having your significant other lie to you. I couldn't fathom why she would do that to us. Wasn't it better to tell the people you love the truth? Despite my confusion over how sudden it all seemed, my mother quickly moved out, and my parents divorced. I wasn't ready for how much my relationship with my mother would change, let alone how it would affect the connection of our whole family. It was like a line was drawn, a "before" and "after." My life before felt whole, normal, complete. Afterwards meant a loneliness I'd never experienced before, crying sessions that felt as if they would never stop.

My father would often talk to me about his negative feelings during this time. I wanted to be someone he could talk to, but it was hard hearing it all. I didn't want to "take sides," despite how disconnected I felt from my mom. Deep down, I had my own sadness and anger that I wasn't addressing or talking about, nor was I asked how I felt. Years later, people would tell me that it was inappropriate for my parents to talk to their children about each other. It's funny what you see as "normal" when you haven't experienced anything different. I thought it was my duty, what I should be doing to be there for them, since I couldn't contribute much else. The worst side effect of not being asked how I felt meant that I truly believed my opinion didn't matter. This horrible trait stuck with me for many years.

For the first time in my life, I had a difficult time making art. I had a college-level art class I was taking, but I didn't want to draw at all. It felt crippling, like a piece of myself was missing. I forced myself to. I *had* to. I didn't want to fail the class. The stress killed my creative spirit, and it seemed to happen all at once. Earlier that year, I remember thinking I was making some of the best art I'd ever made. The boyfriend I had at the time was an artist I admired, who often praised my work. It was a shock to go from that to just three to four months later wanting nothing to do with a pencil and paper. I had to hold onto this for my future. It was the only thing I felt was truly mine, unique to me that nobody could ever take away. Despite feeling it slipping away, I was determined to go to college specifically to continue improving in the art world. It's strange now that I think about it. While I had to force myself to draw back then, it was probably the first time art became "therapy" for me. I put so much emotion into every piece, so much sadness that I couldn't express it aloud. Perhaps art really does imitate life.

My high school graduation was finally over in late May of 2007. It wasn't as exciting as it should have been, since my mom announced soon after that she would be moving across the country to Hawaii. I couldn't fathom, couldn't imagine why she would want to be so far away from us. Did she not want to see me anymore? Did she not love me? At that age, I didn't have much to hang my self-love and self-esteem onto, no "self," anything, really. Parents are meant to usher their children into adulthood. At least, that's how I thought it was supposed to be. Losing her, to me, meant that I didn't have that solid backup anymore. My father stayed and gave us a roof over our heads, but he wasn't someone who shared feelings or worried much about our futures.

Her goodbye in August was unceremonious, with barely any emotion. After that, my self-worth was at an all-time low. I worked in retail to try to save up for a car, for college, for...something? I had no idea what I wanted to do, but money would help no matter what. I didn't want my dad to think I was lazy or wanted to live off him forever. I'd won a small scholarship to a college I wanted to go to, but it would only cover two or three classes. I also didn't have a driver's license or a car, so living on my own didn't seem possible at the time. All these inadequacies felt like they were my fault. Why didn't I have money? Why could I not drive? What hit me later was that those things are *taught*, those things are often achieved through guidance. Something I did not have. I felt I was on my own with no idea how to move forward.

A friend invited me to go to their church, but I refused for a while. Other churches turned me off in the past with what I call "turn or burn" teachings. Basically, they boiled down to "If you don't believe what we believe, you're going to hell." They'd reject any scientific facts, put down others, and generally did not spread love like they preached. In a very desperate moment, I decided to go. My friend was right when he said it was nothing like what I'd experienced before. Their lessons were heartfelt and genuine. They often concentrated on the human side of things, how to treat each other better, while spreading the gospel. One of the lines that stuck with me to this day was when the pastor's voice rang out, "I don't care who you are or what you've done, you're welcome here. I don't care if you've done drugs, if you're an alcoholic, if you're homosexual, if you've cheated, if you've stolen, if you've sinned...you are always welcome in these doors." I'd never heard that preached before, never heard such acceptance, and love up on the pulpit.

I fit in immediately with this church's community. Many friends were made very quickly, people who accepted me and wanted to get to know me. I didn't feel pressured to be anything more than who I was. Singing along with the praise and worship band always filled me with peace. It felt like I was letting out emotions that I couldn't express otherwise, similar to when I would draw. Some nights, the pastor announced an "altar call." Music played, and the front of the pulpit was made available for anyone who needed to come, kneel and allow everyone else to pray over them for whatever was troubling their souls. I'd seen it done many times, but was too afraid to share myself in that intimate way. Finally, one night, I decided I needed to, despite how shy I felt about being up there in front of everyone. With Mom gone, I felt lost and angry. I was so mad at her for leaving us, for leaving me. Those feelings were heavy on my back, as I carried them everywhere with me with no relief. My friends laid their hands on me as I knelt and asked God to take my anger away. To this day, I can't explain how I physically felt those feelings leaking out of my heart. Almost as if I were melting on the inside.

During this time, I was dating someone I considered to be my best friend. From the moment we met, we clicked instantly. Our personalities meshed so well that it felt like we'd known each other for way longer than we had. He soon became the person I turned to for anything and everything, the one I trusted even more than family or friends I'd known longer. We made sense in every way. My adult self feels sheepish to admit, but I saw him as perfect. He was always understanding, calm, and kind, no matter what I did or said. I often tried to pick fights with him, tried to push him away because of how messed up my mind felt. I really thought he was too good to be saddled with someone who had no idea who she was or what she was doing. Throughout it all, he loved me deeply and showed me what unconditional love truly was. Our connection never seemed to waver, through good times and bad. My faith in God and our church grew as did our belief that we were soulmates; it felt as if God made us for each other.

While Mom was gone, she only stayed in touch with my dad, despite his saying he didn't want to speak to her once she left. They had long phone conversations that I sometimes heard when I came home from work. A couple of times, I overheard them talking about my siblings and me. It hurt me when I heard my dad talking about my aimlessness, how all I did was go to my "not real" retail job and hang out with my friends. I lay in bed that night, unable to sleep. What did he expect me to do? I had no money, no help, and no guidance. I knew nothing of the world outside my small piece of it. As the woman I am today, I think I'd confront him as respectfully as I could, ask what he expected if he wasn't going to talk directly to me or help me. I was just an eighteen-year-old whose life got turned upside down. There wasn't a clear path for me at the time, as far as I knew. However, I was heavily influenced by the avoidance my family practised, so instead, I only worried in my own head. I remember making a journal entry, absolutely freaking out: Should I try to get into a college? Should I try to move out? What would make my dad think I was trying enough?

Ironically, this made me spend even more time with my friends outside of my home to distract myself from my heavy thoughts. I missed my mother immensely. Even with her gone, the influence of her and my dad's tumultuous relationship held over me. My boyfriend was very serious about me, to the point of talking about a future for us. I broke up with him a couple of times out of fear. I thought that if we reached marriage, if we depended on each other as my parents had, we'd end up fighting and resenting each other. I didn't want our relationship ruined by that pressure. Any kind of commitment like that scared me. I'd have strong feelings but wouldn't want to act on them. This led to me feeling paralysed and not working towards any sort of future for myself. The most I did was save money as often as I could with my meagre pay so that I could become more independent by buying a car.

Church really inspired my art at this time and for years to come. There's so much rich imagery in Christianity, and it frequently showed up in my drawings. I was already obsessed with drawing wings of any sort, so angels were an easy connection made as well. To this day, I still draw wings wherever I can. It was a very productive time for my creativity; I even wrote a short story, titled "Seven Feathers." It was my first attempt at writing as an art form, versus just venting to my private journal. Sadly, it reflected my mental health at this time: scattered, immature, and lacking stability. And that's not a terrible thing! First drafts are always a little unkempt (I'm being generous; that first draft was A LOT of unkempt). I never edited it, never looked at it again after my boyfriend read it. I was too scared to try anything more than the minimum. Maybe on some level, because of my lack of adult guidance, I felt that was all I could ever do: write or draw in my little room, then leave it in a corner to collect dust. Not to shame anyone who loves those hobbies and only does it for themselves. I'd always wanted more when I was younger, but where was that ambition just a couple of years later? It had been drained out of me by all of the emotional turmoil I was going through.

However, my life was turned upside down again by my mother deciding to come back home, and more specifically, to live with us. For the first time in a year, I had contact with her as she asked my siblings and me if we would be okay with her coming back to live with us. I pushed my feelings down, just as my siblings probably did, and said that it was fine. The behaviour my parents displayed was baffling, but I felt I had no right to comment. I felt like a "kid" couldn't comment on the parents' decisions, despite how uncomfortable I was. Even worse, I drained my savings to help with her expenses to move back. It wasn't much by any means, but I had to start over again from scratch. My dad eventually paid me back in his own way by buying me a computer, though that didn't exactly replace the money I'd saved up for something else that seemed more important at the time. Familial duty won out; I didn't think about what I needed, but rather what my family needed, even the one I hadn't seen in a very long time. In my mind, my family would be "whole" again.

Adjusting to life once she was back had a lot of challenges. It felt weird with her around again. My boyfriend made sense of it for me by saying, "I think it's because in your head, she isn't your mom anymore. She's like this stranger who's very comfortable with you, but she isn't the mom that left." It validated my discomfort. I barely wanted to touch or hug her. Also, this had five of us living in a small, three-bedroom apartment, often feeling cramped. It clearly wasn't enough space for all of us. I tried as hard as I could to function normally: work, sleep, see my friends, save money, rinse, and repeat.

Having my boyfriend, the community at my church, and my friends helped tremendously, as they made me feel like I had somewhere that I belonged. When I didn't show up for a service, I had friends saying they'd missed me. I felt I had two halves of a life: one in my boyfriend's town, where those friends lived, and then another life where my old childhood friends and family were. Sometimes the two came together, and it brought me joy to introduce everyone. In fact, some of those connections still exist today. Meanwhile, my living situation changed many times over the next four years. I even ended up living with just my mother at one point in our own little apartment, mostly due to my parents' usual fighting and wanting to separate. While I still had my own feelings to sort out, my mother gave me more freedom than my father. As a nineteen/twenty-year-old with a very active social life, that was valuable to me. She gave me trust that I felt my dad never gave me. We all ended up living together again after a while. I was told it was for financial reasons. Even at this stage, I had an odd sense of relief at having my "whole" family together again, though my sister had moved out by that point with her boyfriend. I often wonder if it was an old leftover childhood feeling, viewing my family as "better" or "whole" despite how unhappy my parents seemed to be when living together. I can't really blame my past self since they kept returning to that same situation of their own free will.

My boyfriend continued to plan our future, and I continued the trend of being terrified of the commitment. My brain kept imagining us ending up like my parents. One day, I saw a random commercial that finally changed my perspective. I can't even remember what the commercial was for. Two adults, a man and a woman, stood in a kitchen together, washing dishes. They were laughing while helping each other with the simple task. The camera turned to show their young daughter watching them without them knowing. A narrator spoke of how children watched when you didn't think they were and were affected by your actions. It dawned on me: *I* was that child. I watched my parents for years, absorbed their fights and erratic behaviours, and believed that was how my life was going to be. I decided I wanted to live differently, stop being the influenced child and instead grow into my own woman, free of what I saw my whole life. Soon after, I declared my love and commitment to my boyfriend, and we purchased promise rings together. We wore those rings every day for the next few years, sure that we were going to be married and spend our lives together.

That's when my "future," or what you could call my narrow-minded view of a "future," became clear to me. I worked at various retail jobs for the next three years, hung out with my friends, went to church, and saved up money as I usually did. Now, however, it felt as if it had a purpose: my boyfriend was the silver lining. I was going to wait for him to be done with college, and then I'd move out of my parents' house with him. Soon after, we'd get married and start our lives. I thought of no individual ambition, only that one goal. This plan didn't even have steps; I was just waiting on someone else. Looking back at it now, it makes me sad. I should have been working towards my own dreams. Art was still a lifeblood for me; it always had been. But then, as soon as I was done with a drawing, it sat in my sketchbook, only seen by a few friends if I posted it on social media. Gone were my teenage dreams of being a writer or illustrator. This really shows me how much I hadn't truly grown up yet. My brain had one breakthrough on its own, and somehow that made me think I had everything figured out. It makes sense now, looking back. I was only nineteen, and people's brains don't fully develop until their mid-twenties. Without adult guidance or someone to give me advice to push for my own goals, I was content to "survive," day by day and wait for that magical, unrealistic happy ending.

The optimism for this future didn't last forever. After years of waiting, family drama, and other friends moving forward in their lives, I began to feel depressed. At the time, I didn't know what exactly it was. It just felt like a heavy, vague sense of dissatisfaction. In early 2012, I had some conversations with my boyfriend about it. It seemed as if all of my time was either taken up by work or hanging out with him whenever possible. Our schedules had a hard time lining up, since my job's hours were so random and he had a job and went to college, so it felt like any free time was always obligated to each other. He asked if I wanted to break up. Of course I didn't! I think I just needed *more*, though I had no idea what 'more' I wanted. I hadn't contemplated what I wanted, really wanted out of life, in years. We concluded that maybe giving me an off

day to myself every now and then may help. Perhaps the precious time to myself would help me figure out what my individual goals were as he took care of his own. That plan never came to fruition. A month later, on a work shift no less, I was questioned by the police concerning my boyfriend. I cried on the phone to him afterwards in the breakroom, demanding answers. He said to go home and that he'd tell me everything.
Telling me everything never happened.

My perspective of him was absolutely shattered, so I broke up with him. How could the person I trusted the most, more than my family and friends, who I'd known longer than him, be the one to betray me more than anyone else in my life? He portrayed himself as honest, genuine, and Godly. My naive mind believed him to be almost perfect. Everything I said, he understood. Our sense of humour was nearly the same. He was comforting and kind, not just to me, but to everyone around him. Any flaws I saw were minimal, practically nonexistent.

After the lies, it made me wonder…was the person I saw really him? Was he wearing a mask around me, hiding the man he truly was underneath? And I'd fallen hard for it, dedicated my life to him and only him.

Finally, I decided to take hold of my life and go after my own dreams. I used my work's insurance to seek therapy, did even more art for myself, and learned more about mental health and self-care.

Just kidding.

I wish that's what I could write in earnest. My young brain wasn't educated on mental health or self-care. All I knew was survival mode, which meant dating again almost immediately to distract myself from the pain. It didn't work then, nor did it work as I went forward. My mother told me that I acted as if I were "sick," and I suppose she was right. I was sick; sick at heart, sick in my mind, and deeper, perhaps even down to my soul. I had no idea how to deal with what happened other than blindly pushing forward, pretending that everything was fine. It was the technique I was taught by example while growing up. The one positive was that I'd built a loyal group of friends over the years. While I did desperately need therapy and better self-care, I at least had many people who loved me to turn to. Despite any hardships with my family during this time, they still had my back and tried to take care of me in their own ways. I was lucky that I hadn't gotten married to this man or moved in together as we'd previously planned. True colours will show someday in one way or another.

As I pushed myself through that year, I decided I needed new people in my life. Not just new romantic partners, but new friends as well. Since the breakup left quite a hole in my life, I thought that perhaps I should let others in and try to learn to trust again. I stopped going to church since I didn't want to see my ex-boyfriend. This meant I lost many friends I'd made for years, and I had a huge crisis of faith. Many of my other friends were getting engaged or in serious relationships, so I saw them less than I used to. These new friends were more on my level of life: a bit lost, working hard, and trying to find their way. It was nice to laugh and forget everything for a while when I was with them. Even better, one of those friends also loved to draw, so we'd often spend days together drawing at the park or in her apartment. This encouraged my art therapy once more. We made art constantly. She said later that I made some of my best art that year, since the emotions she saw in them were so raw.

It's funny what a mix of good and bad just one year can be. 2012 was a turning point in my life, but I didn't take the opportunities that were laid out before me. I was free to concentrate on myself, but I didn't see that as important. My focus was getting back what I had: a life partner, someone else to concentrate on. That ended in me jumping into a relationship far sooner than I was ready to. It became serious enough that I moved in with him and my art friend a few months after we started dating. Looking back, I admit I was mainly trying to escape my family home. The turmoil never ended between my parents, and I was usually stuck in the middle. At age twenty-three, I moved out, hoping to start a life away from the constant negativity my household brought.

When actions aren't made in good faith, I learned they don't seem to work out very well. My move wasn't thought out at all, so, of course, my romantic relationship and friendship with my roommate ended in disaster. Before, I thought it was good to have friends on "my level."

However, I came to find that it's better to surround yourself with people who can teach you something, who are doing things that you want to achieve someday. I ended up taking care of these people to a certain extent. I always felt I had to be the mature and levelheaded one, since my boyfriend and friend often had emotional meltdowns and fights among themselves. I went from one unstable home life to another. I began to hate who I was and who I'd become. Here I was, wasting my twenties, barely surviving, and not doing anything. Literally anything, like I'd done for years. I went to my retail job, came home, and mostly distracted myself by scrolling on my laptop.

During these years, I found myself drawing a certain character over and over. She was always dressed in elaborate costumes and goggles that hid her face, almost as if she were trying to hide. Words usually surrounded her, either in my own writing or in newspaper clippings I would glue around her. I soon realised that she was my emotional outlet, someone who represented me and all the feelings I didn't express in my daily life. When I posted drawings of her on my social media, she seemed to impact anyone who saw her. Many had huge compliments for the style and power of the words I selected. One friend even told me that he really felt she had a story behind her. Even as repressed as I felt, my art found a way. Self-expression will always find a way, even when you aren't trying.

After my inevitable breakup, I moved back in with my parents. Back to square one. This time period was the worst I'd ever felt in my life. I'd given so much of myself to others and had little left for myself. My teenage years and my twenties were solely dedicated to concentrating on my family, friends, and boyfriends. I'd somehow pushed myself and my needs and wants away into a dusty corner, never to be looked at again. This is exactly what I needed, though: to really, truly face myself, flaws and all. While I could look back and point the finger at this or that, ultimately, it was time to accept what had happened to me and start the healing process. Not for anyone else, but only for myself. I remember so many times lying in bed, staring at my parents' ceiling, as my thoughts raced over the choices I'd made. It was time to make different ones, better ones. It was time for a change.

First, I asked my parents for guidance on buying a car. I'd saved up enough for a decent down payment, and I wanted to be sure I was going to get a good deal. At least doing basically nothing for two to three years allowed for that. With reliable transportation secured, I was more independent than I'd ever been. Second, I decided that I would do my absolute best at work, even if I didn't like my job. This attitude adjustment landed me a promotion quickly, which helped me enough monetarily to move out of my parents' house in just a few short months. I chose two friends I'd had for years to move in with. I wasn't going to rush into moving in with a romantic partner again.

During this transformative phase in my life, I craved the comfort of the ex-boyfriend who had betrayed me years ago. I was so angry with myself for it, but I also couldn't help how I felt. He'd moved out of the state the year before and come back for a visit, where we spent a whole day together. We caught up on the years we missed in each other's lives. It strangely felt like no time had passed; our natural connection was still strong, despite everything. All I'd wanted was him for so long. I thought perhaps us getting back together would "fix" what was broken within me. Maybe, just maybe, he was the missing piece I mistakenly rid myself of. I often wondered if I was wrong for not forgiving him. At this time, I hated who I'd become. The last time I remembered liking myself was when I was with him.

However, at the moment when he confessed that he was moving back home in a few months and asked if we could start over, I said no. I was done living for someone else, done with thinking that other people were going to be the solution to my life's problems. I'd made so much progress, and I decided that going back to him would be living in the past instead of embracing my future. It was a major turning point for me. True healing was what I needed, not a Band-Aid, and I finally understood that.

My mind felt clear for the first time in years. I didn't know exactly what my future held, but it was going to be new and different. I already made some healthy decisions for myself, and those continued. Over the next couple of years, I started working at an office job, finally ridding myself of retail, something I never thought I was good enough for without a college degree. I arranged visits with a primary care doctor with the insurance that came with the job and spoke to her about my depression and anxiety. The medicine she prescribed helped immensely. Many feel that these actions mean you are admitting failure. It is quite the opposite. Taking care of your mental health allows you to do more with your life, to feel better and achieve more. Failure is not even close to what I was feeling after getting the help I'd desperately needed for years.

Therapy came next. She helped me name and identify many stressful behaviours and habits I'd developed. For many years, I felt my hurt and traumas weren't as "hard" as other people's, that I was just weak. She validated me and gently guided me through ways to accept everything, while also continuing to take care of myself physically and mentally. Therapy even unlocked a few memories my brain must have shut out for my own safety. I'd excused a person I trusted sexually violating me because I was young. After all, I thought "men were just like that." The person probably doesn't even remember this, but I do. While these memories are painful even to this day, they helped me truly move on and let go of a lot of things. It showed me how much my trust and naivety were taken advantage of, and I was ready to grow past it all.

Through all of this, my creativity blossomed. Drawings poured out of me. I even tried different ideas and styles, but I always seemed to come back to that particular character I mentioned earlier. It was so therapeutic to come up with different ways to draw her: her body disintegrating into shreds of paper, words written on every inch of the page, thanks to asking friends for phrases or song lyrics they liked, even burning the edges of the paper in one piece (which was particularly scary). She was more than my emotional outlet. She had her own story, and I finally decided to write it. Therapy through my art over the years got me through so many hard, lonely nights. When all else failed, drawing my feelings and writing in my journal helped me organise my thoughts and express my emotions in a healthy, meaningful way. Now it was time to share it with whoever I could through the fictional story of this character, who I soon named Jayde. Young adult books impacted my creativity all throughout my life, and I wrote my first novel, titled Sin Eater, to honour them.

Sin Eater is for all youths who feel lost and hopeless, who may have nobody solid in their lives to guide them. Children often look to the adults in their lives to show them the way. How else do we learn, other than observation of the ones around us that we feel "know better" than us? I floated aimlessly for a great portion of my life. Bad memories and past trauma controlled my life for a long time, and my journey for the main character of Sin Eater, Jayde, seems to reflect that without me even trying. I've found that your story will come out in some way, no matter what. It's in the choices you make, how you treat others, and what you do going forward. I finally chose myself, and I was privileged enough to have access to medicine and therapy. Not all do.

It's why I preach therapy in other ways, like my art therapy. Drawing your feelings can be extremely empowering. Despite any wavering on my part, art was always there for me. It doesn't need anything fancy: often I only had lined notebook paper and an ink pen. I drew what I wanted, what represented myself at the time. A journal helped as well. I wrote my rawest feelings into it, my therapist, who just happened not to talk back. Maybe I wasn't getting advice, but I emptied all the negativity I had within me. Plus, I could look back at this written record and give myself a way to remember good times, despite any bad ones I wrote about. Now I write fiction, a perfect way to reach out to others through fantasy yet still teach the lessons I learned throughout my years. I want our youth to know that I understand their struggles, to acknowledge how important they are to not just their own friends and family, but to the future of our world.

I'm so glad I didn't lose touch with art.

Whether it's drawing, writing, dancing, singing, crafting, sewing, tattooing...anything creative, please do it. Not for anyone else, but for yourself. Let it fill your spirit and inspire you. It's what makes us whole, in a lot of ways. It's how we show others who we are in the purest way. I'm currently trying to share my first novel as much as I can while writing its sequel, and I have plans for others. My art will hopefully continue to be hung in various places, since I've found some around my city willing to do so. The ambition and drive that I had when I was young is back, and I never want it to disappear again. I'm more independent and powerful than ever, and anyone else can be too if they take steps to take care of their beautiful minds.

As of now, my life is full of healthy relationships, thanks to all the helpful steps I've mentioned. I met a man, my now husband Shan, who really helped guide me to independence and confidence. He always encourages me to try new things and to go for my dreams, effortlessly believing in me when I don't believe in myself. My trust issues often reared their ugly head over the years. It's extremely tough to get past relationship trauma, even when you are with a good person. Therapy and his understanding were a recipe that kept us going strong to this day, though. Meanwhile, my parents are remarried. I had my own feelings about this for a while, but through healthy mental practices, I realised that their decisions and anyone else's decisions are not my own. Therefore, I will be as good a daughter and person as I can be, and love with all I have. My relationship with them is the best it's ever been, peaceful, loving, and always there for each other. I know I can count on them. I'm also blessed with a fantastic group of loyal friends, people I've been close with for many years. I don't know who or where I'd be without them.

As for my faith, I have yet to figure it out. I haven't attended any churches since I stopped going to my old one back in 2012. It was the only one I'd ever connected with in my life, so others had a lot to live up to. Honestly, I'm content with where I'm at since I feel it's all about the journey. My life is rich and full of wonderful people and goals. Perhaps someday things will change, but for now, I am fulfilled spiritually without a church or religion.

Mental health awareness will always be important to me. Every book I write will reflect these messages. I always thought I hadn't done anything "great," but I have. Pulling yourself out of a dark place is one of the single most amazing things a human being can do for themselves, and for others. Never doubt how amazing you are, and how much your art can impact others to believe in themselves, too. I'll keep going and never stop trying. I owe it to the young girl I once was, watching Sailor Moon and drawing feverishly, hoping someday my art could tell such an inspiring story.

# Women I'm Inspired By

*Naoko Takeuchi (Takeuchi Naoko properly in Japan)*
Naoko is a comic writer and illustrator from Japan. She most notably created the comic Sailor Moon in 1992, which has also been adapted as an anime, video games, and other live action television shows. Her work always features strong women, loyal friends, and the strength of heart. To this day, her art and storytelling have impacted my own in the best ways.

*Lauren Oliver*
Lauren Oliver is an American author from Queens, New York. Her award winning novels have been translated into more than thirty languages. Her work has even been adapted into a movie and a television show. They often feature women protagonists of varying ages, so any woman reading can find something to relate to. Her stories show complicated, human relationships that tug at the heartstrings and make the reader think. I fell in love with her prose instantly, and it ultimately inspired me to write my own book.

# Reflections

## Sarah Wright
## England

Single mother of one, Sarah Wright gained her MSc in Criminal Justice and Criminology at the age of thirty-five, after gaining her BSc in Forensic Psychology at the age of thirty-four, after leaving school at the age of fourteen with no qualifications. Her study, which focused on employers' perceptions and attitudes towards the hiring of ex-offenders in the construction industry, is the second one of its kind in the academic world of writing, earning a distinction from the University of Derby.

Having been through the criminal justice system after being used by the police to gain a conviction of her abuser. She understands what it means to be discriminated against for having a criminal record when trying to obtain employment, which is why she has created Second Chance Recruitment, an organisation which takes ex-offenders through a "prison to employment rehabilitation" recruitment process.

She hopes that her story can help individuals all over the world who are currently or have in the past endured domestic violence to realise they are worthy and there is support available; not to mention a huge, bright light at the end of the tunnel waiting for that moment they find that last little bit of hope, courage and strength to say fuck this, fuck you, and fuck yeah!

To discover more about Sarah, please visit
https://secondchance-recruitment.co.uk
https://facebook.com/secondchance-recruitment

# This Thing Called Life

*"Where do I start?"* Well, as far back as I can recall, my life has felt like a tumbleweed of shit rolling uncontrollably down a vertical hill, with jagged glass and boulders obstructing the path, causing turmoil, pain, and scars on its never-ending way down.

Born on February 12, 1987, at Queens Medical Centre in Nottingham, my mother was alone in the delivery room. My father was in the pub at the time of my birth, which does not surprise me at all. It was an all-too-familiar occurrence throughout my childhood, him being at the pub. As I look back now and understand my childhood from an adult's perspective, I suspect my mother was not too overjoyed that day. I imagine she was compassionate and gentle, yet worried and deflated. My dad treated her terribly. He was unfaithful, physically and mentally abusive, even to the point where he had pushed her out of a window when she was pregnant. He even threw a concrete slab through my nana's house window. I was one year old when he left, and I cannot help but imagine what my mother would have gone through and the childhood I would have had if he hadn't.

He emptied the council house, which they bought together, leaving my mum with two children. A wooden chair was the only thing he left behind - in the middle of an empty living room. No wonder, as the years went by, my mum and I had no maternal bond. I no longer resent my mum for this as I understand what she went through. She had to do what she had to do to ensure we all survived, even if it was at my unknowing expense. I had counselling when I was thirty-one; it really helped me put that behind me at last. Lucky for me and my siblings, my mum met my stepdad, who is loving and caring, and I still have a great relationship with him to this day, despite my mum and him being separated. He moved in and contributed to the upbringing of me, my brother, and my sister.

That being said, the damage was done, and from around twelve years old, I would shout at the top of my voice, "I cannot wait till I am sixteen! I am out of here!" Looking back now, I still do not understand why, at that age, I felt so strongly about getting away from the only family I had, especially with nowhere to go. My theory is the lack of bond with my mother, my stepdad not being my 'real' dad, and my real dad being an aggressive control freak - someone who I only pretended to listen to due to the fear of being beaten or intimidated, I was scared to even breathe, never mind speak my truth.

At fourteen years of age, I started to ditch school and hang around with a few girls I had met. The five of us were inseparable, and our days consisted of managing not to attend school without our parents finding out. We'd meet up, put our dinner money together to buy cigarettes and weed, then hide out in the woods or at each other's houses. We'd do anything so as not to get caught skiving. I soon began to realise I was not like these girls. At that time, they were more street-wise, from city urban areas, clued up and were sexually active from as young as thirteen. I was naïve, shy, lacked any confidence, a virgin and had low self-esteem. I was a child with no life experience, no teachings, and no academic achievements. I'd struggled my whole way through school due to undiagnosed dyslexia, and I left at fifteen - before I got expelled. With no direction, no conventional teachings and feeling as I'd had no one who cared about me, I was a recipe for disaster. Imagine putting all that in a bowl, mixing it around a few times, adding all the bad things you could ever imagine you have in today's society, with fake, manipulative, and evil individuals, thrown into the mix for good measure. Yep, you have the perfect recipe for a fucking nightmare of a time.

I literally went from a child thinking the world was Barbies, rainbows, and candy floss, to realising it was drugs, guns, men, and madness.

However, I had no choice. It was too late. There was no turning back, nowhere to go, and no one who wanted me, because at this point, my mum hated me thanks to all the angry outbursts and damage I'd caused to the house. I'd kicked my bedroom door off its hinges many times and thrown all my belongings out the windows; never mind the verbal abuse she had to endure from me. No wonder she'd had enough.

A week before my sixteenth birthday, I'd gone back to my mum's home to collect my clothes as I was going to stay with a friend whose mum worked away and would come home to fill the fridge so we could eat. We got into an argument over where I'd been and why I'd not been home or called anyone. I didn't care. I didn't care about myself, never mind anyone else, so I told my mum where to go and to leave me alone. As I turned and walked out the front door, I remember turning around at the gate to my mum charging at me like a raging bull with a brick in her hand. I began to run, then turned to look behind me and started laughing at her. Then I was gone. I sat in a car with two older men I knew from the streets who were well known and at least ten years older than me. I said, "What the fuck am I going to do? I have nowhere to go! I have nothing! I am fucked!" We all started to brainstorm, and they made a phone call, turned to me, and said, "Right, we have another girl like you who works for us. We've put her in a flat and you can stay there with her." I was really grateful, but also really stupid. How could I not see that this offer would come at a price?

*"Silly, slow, dumb, stupid, naïve, Sarah"*. The men drove me to a flat and introduced me to the girl, who was a few years older than me, and who was visibly someone who was used to this life. It was also obvious she'd been assigned to use me to both her advantage and theirs. But I didn't mind; I had nothing else to do, and I needed to learn the ways of this new world as thoroughly and as quickly as possible to survive. Which I did.

I lived there for around six months, driving around with her in the passenger seat of her car, as she followed orders and ran errands all day, making sure to secure the rent due on the flat, and food to live. After a while, the neighbours reported us to the police about the activities and visitors to the flat regularly. This resulted in us being evicted, so I moved back to my mum's as I had nowhere else to go. The day before eviction, all the lads who were around our age, and who worked for the older men, came round, had a party, and graffiti-ed all the walls.

I was seventeen at the time and had been seeing a guy who was around twenty-seven. I found out I was pregnant, which was a huge shock to me, as I believed I could not get pregnant due to my lifestyle, which consisted of smoking weed and taking pills to numb the pain of my miserable existence. Upon realising the situation I was in, with nowhere to live, no money, no support, and the fact I had nothing to offer myself or the baby, I decided to have an abortion. This was the most difficult decision of my life; my mum had raised us in church with the principles of Christianity. I knew and felt it was wrong, believed God would be disappointed in me, but I felt I had no choice. I went to the hospital, went through the procedure, then my partner picked me up and took me home. Two hours later, I passed another baby. The nurses had failed to tell me I was pregnant with twins.

My whole world fell apart, and I attempted suicide as I could not live with the guilt of my actions. I broke down, fell to my knees, whilst shoving tablets down my throat. My mum and friend held me down trying to stop me from ending this thing called life. I needed to get away from Nottingham, from all the people - and more importantly, this version of myself. After my suicide attempt, my mum called my nana, who lived in Loughborough, to ask if I could stay with her. Thankfully, she said yes, and I packed the little belongings I had, and I went to stay with my nan. The next day, I applied for a job in the local pub and started to work there every day, doing my best to save some money. Some of the people I knew still contacted me and stayed in touch.

After around a year living with my nan, I moved back to Nottingham. "Big Mistake" and once again, I found myself moving into another flat with the same girl doing the same bullshit to survive. A few months passed, and I'd gone out to meet some friends and ended up talking to a guy. We quickly became close. I know now that it was because I was damaged and distorted, still had low self-worth and no confidence. I must have come with a big neon sign above my head about how damaged I was because he sank his devil's claws in so fast without me even realising it. I would stay over at his place most nights and pretty much abandoned the flat I was in. I didn't really see any red flags at this time, but to be honest, identifying red flags was not one of my strong points, so why would I?

One day, I got a phone call from the landlord of the flat I'd abandoned, stating the police were there, and that I needed to get there immediately to remove my belongings. He'd had enough - and who could blame him? I collected my stuff and moved in with my new boyfriend. *"boyfriend"* What? Who? When did this happen? It was then I realised I was fucked again.

He began to control every aspect of my life. I wasn't allowed friends, a phone to call anyone, nor was I allowed to see my family or have my own money. I wasn't allowed my own opinion or a voice of any kind. Asking questions was impossible, and to him, I was an invisible slave allowed to do only what he said. Being forced to cook three meals a day at the age of nineteen when I'd never been taught to cook was hard. I ate at the local sandwich shop, which people from Nottingham call 'the cob shop'. I ate there every morning for breakfast, at other food shops in the evening or at friends' houses. I had never cooked a meal in my life before this point. The 'boyfriend' got his mum to come for the weekend from London to teach me how to cook, just for him to be satisfied. I'd clean the house every day, ready for his inspection - just to make sure it was up to his standards. He'd come home and run his finger over plug sockets, checking for dust. I became paranoid about cleaning, looking for dirt and dust all the time just to avoid his abusive behaviour. No longer having freedom over any aspect of my life, I existed for the sole purpose of being and doing whatever he needed and wanted me to do.

Once a week, he would say, "Right, you have an hour to go and treat yourself. Here is some money. Driving the car he gave me, I went to a clothing shop to buy something to 'reward myself' for all the hard work of cooking and cleaning I'd done that week. *"Thanks dickhead"* What an amazing, kind person you are "not". Even the car he'd given me was because he'd taken my car, made it his, then sold it. One day, I asked to go to the shop. The queue at the till was longer than expected, which meant I took longer than he'd anticipated. I left the shop panicking, rushing, and trying to come up with a suitable scenario that would reduce the abuse I would get once I got back. Walking through the door, he questioned me and accused me of sleeping with someone else. Insults continued throughout the rest of the day, insults such as "slag". Eventually, he grabbed me, punched both my legs repeatedly so hard that I could barely walk.. After the beating, he sent me to my room to *'sort myself out'* because I was crying and *"looked ugly"*. I went to my room and started to strangle myself with the tie from my dressing gown. I couldn't take this anymore. The pain I inflicted on myself somehow took away the pain he was causing.

Then something inside me snapped. The pain I was causing myself somehow gave me the strength to say, "You can do this, Sarah." Then I told myself, "I didn't do anything wrong to deserve this. Nothing! I just went to the shop." Once I'd managed to find the strength to calm down and stop crying, I made myself look presentable. When I was allowed back downstairs, I had to pretend I was ok, and everything was fine. *"Yes, Sir. How many bags full, Sir?".* The physical and mental abuse became more frequent, and there was not a day that went by that I did not get a backhander round the face for saying a word he did not agree with. This became my reality.

As an individual who had no self-worth, self-esteem, or self-confidence, I felt as though I deserved this. I cared more about his feelings than I did about my own. Constantly asking if he was okay, if he needed anything, and trying to judge what mood he was in so as not to get hit or shouted at. He had completely broken me to a point I would tell myself daily, "as long as my family are ok, I can endure this forever," But they were not okay.

On my twenty-first birthday, my family had arranged a large get-together with family and friends, all having a meal together. My boyfriend had been out all day, and I was not able to contact him. I thought, "Right, I'll pop to Tesco to get some Valentine's gifts, not realising he'd returned home when I was out. He went mental because he was home before me. He hit me, threatened to shave my hair off, and stabbed me six times in my back with a car key. At that point, I heard someone knocking on the door. It was my stepdad. He'd come to collect me to take me to the family meal. I arrived and looked over to see my whole family sitting there. Rushing into the bathroom in my old clothes, as I'd not had a chance to get ready, my mum and aunty came in and closed the door behind me. I broke down and told them everything I was going through, what had been happening, what he'd done. I told them to call an ambulance as I was having a mental breakdown. My mind was overrun with worry, confusion, and turmoil, thinking he is going to go crazy, as I have now told my family, for the first time in over a year, what I have been experiencing. As usual, I put on a brave face and sat through a five-course meal with twelve members of my family, pretending once again that everything was ok.

After the meal, I stayed at my mum's house as my stepdad told me, "You are not going back there!". In the morning, the door was knocking, and I was petrified. It was him asking for me, and my stepdad said, "She doesn't want to see you." Less than an hour later, he smashed all my mum's windows and her car to pieces. We all had to move out, so we went and stayed at my nan's house, where he couldn't find us, until we could figure out what to do. Sitting in my nan's living room, the phone rang, and she passed it to me. It was the police. A male officer stated his name and said, "it is very important you do not repeat any of this conversation." I said, "what do you want?" He answered, "we know what he has done, and we want you to tell us everything," I asked him if he was to protect my whole family, at which point he went silent. Through fear, I told him, "Do not call back, just leave us alone. This whole time, the police were well aware of everything he was doing to me, but not once did they try to help." They were more concerned with securing a conviction against him than helping me. Looking back now, I can believe they had the power to stop him and stop all the pain he had caused other victims, yet they let him continue to rain terror on innocent people, making sure they would get the conviction they desperately wanted.

As the weeks went by, my family and I had to move in with my uncle, who lived on the outskirts of Nottingham, for our safety. We also had to wait until the repairs had been completed at my mum's house. During this time, he'd been to other family members' homes, threatening them, whilst looking for me. A few weeks passed, and I suppose he'd calmed down, come back to reality and the realisation of what he'd done, as he apologised and gave my mum all the money needed to fix the damage he'd caused. Until this day, I cannot explain why I did this, but I woke up one morning at my uncle's and thought to myself, "I cannot do this no more." And I went back to him - the biggest mistake I've ever made in my life. I disregarded everything he'd done to me and my family and put his feelings first once again. Something my mother has never forgiven me for, even up until this day, seventeen years later. *"Can you really blame her?"* My only explanation for such a horrendous decision would be to look at it from a psychological stance. Taking into consideration the physical and mental abuse I'd endured for a long period of time; I'd not realised I was suffering from a case of *Stockholm syndrome: "A deep bond between a victim and abuser developing a strong sense of loyalty despite the damage caused to themselves".*

A few months passed, and I was right back into the routine I knew, being controlled and dictated to daily. One morning, we woke up to a loud bang and shouting at the door. I looked out of the window, and it was the police. We both contemplated what to do, and he said, "Open the door to them before they kick it off!" The undercover officer stood at the door and said to me, "Sarah, shut the fuck up! Where is he?" Then, around six officers barged their way into the house, keeping me in the living room as two plainclothes officers went upstairs and arrested him. He was taken out of the house, and off they went, leaving me with the plainclothes officers as they searched the house high and low. I could overhear them talking, and recall one of them saying, "nine hundred pounds for a pair of fucking shoes". They took both cars and all their belongings out of the house and left. I was left with nothing. No phone to contact anyone, no money, and no transport to go anywhere. I remember being scared and nervous, yet relieved he was gone. Time passed, and he was remanded into custody.

Beyond my knowledge, he'd been committing many different crimes, ranging from robbery, blackmail, attempted murder, and had fifteen separate charges against him. Silly me, I was thinking, "This is it; it is over. I am free." How far from the truth that was! As the days passed, I was now his personal jail assistant, being fed orders to get this, do that, and go here. My life now consisted of sitting at home smoking weed to numb my pointless existence and constant prison visits. Another month passed, and I received information from his solicitor that the police wanted to speak with me voluntarily. They wanted to interview me and gave me a day and time to go to the police station. I remember not being worried or concerned, as I had not done anything wrong, so I was a little confused as to what they wanted. I thought it was just to ask me questions about his circumstances. The morning of the interview arrived, and I got up, got dressed and drove to the police station. Leaving the new car he'd bought me (so I could make visits to the prison to see him) outside the police station, I went in to meet my solicitor. I had to give them my belongings, and I was then held in an interview room. Two officers entered, introduced themselves and continued to ask me questions. Upon the advice of my solicitor, and the fact that I did not trust the police due to past experiences, I answered, "no comment". They knew about the abuse I was enduring, yet chose not to take that into consideration, and now they wanted me to comment. They asked numerous questions in regard to his charges and other victims, which I knew nothing about. I was not allowed to leave the house without permission, have a phone, or have contact with family and friends - never mind knowing anything else! After around an hour of continuous questions and me repeating, "no comment", they left the room. reappeared, they reappeared and said, "we are now going to charge you with robbery and two counts of perverting the cause of justice." I responded with, "hmmm, ok, well, I have no idea what that is, but whatever." *Silly Sarah".* I remember thinking, "Well, I've done nothing wrong, so I'm going home. Also, I've never been in trouble with the police before and have a clean record. I'll be fine." Oh, how wrong I was!

They locked me in a cell from 9 am Friday until Monday morning, only bringing me out to question me for hours and hours, over and over for three days, only for them to hear, "no comment." Why should I tell them anything, even if I knew? Look at the way they treat victims! The way they had treated me! I was in no state to think straight. I was in a state of fear and survival mode for myself and my family. Monday morning came around, and a female officer came to my cell. I recall her being very nice and caring towards me; the first person to treat me like a human in three days. She helped me get a shower and provided me with clean clothes as I had to attend court. You only had to look at me and see something wasn't right. I weighed around seven stone, being five foot eight, I had not eaten for three days and was visibly having a mental breakdown. I struggled to comprehend what was happening to me, and how someone who has been getting abused for over a year - by a known monster - could be treated this way - especially by the people who knew what was happening and are supposed to protect us all as citizens. "Thanks".

I arrived at the court and sat in the glass dock, peering over, I could see my mum and the anguished look on her face. *This absolutely broke my heart, but I had to stay strong and show strength to ensure she did not worry even more.*

The solicitors and judge went back and forth, and I remember them discussing my bail conditions. It was really difficult for me to understand what was being said. No surprises there! I had the academic level of education of a twelve-year-old and the social skills to match. My family and I were on the edge of our seats waiting for the bail decision. For a second, it seemed as though it had been granted, and I saw the look of relief on my mum's face, then in a split second, I heard I was to be remanded in custody. My mum broke down, and I looked at her and said, "It's okay, don't worry. I'll be fine." My mum loved me. She is a good person with a kind heart, something I've never disputed or doubted. We've just had a complicated relationship and found it impossible to connect.

Handcuffed by the court officers and then taken downstairs to be put in a holding cell, I had to wait for the Group Four bus to arrive to take me to prison. I got on the bus, and there was another girl on it. I remember asking her what it was like, trying to take it all in and prepare myself. It felt like it took forever to get there, and at one point, the bus got lost and had to pull over to ask for directions. It was pitch black outside, and I had no idea what was happening. Then, when we finally arrived and I saw the sign, *"Welcome to HMP Peterborough. We hope you enjoy your stay"* I walked up to the desk, stated my name, and was put in a holding cell while I waited to get processed. In the cell were two other girls who proceeded to stare at each other, then at me. They stood up and, in an intimidating manner, said, "What have you got?" I said, "What?" They said, "What have you got on you?" That's when I realised *"they are banging it on my toes"*, meaning *'I am about to get beaten up and bullied'* as they think I have drugs on me. I looked them dead in the face and said, "I know I look like a crack head right now because I've been in cells for three days, but I don't have anything on me. All I do is smoke weed, so don't ask me any fucking questions!". They sat down and didn't say another word. At that point, I was barely holding on to my sanity, so I was the last person to try and fuck with. I was empty and numb inside, and there was nothing anyone could say or do to me that was worse than what I'd been enduring, or what I was going through. *"God strike me down now if I'm lying, but there's no way on this planet I'm getting bullied in here"*. That was a great practice run and learning a drill for what was about to be my reality - and my life for the next eight months. *"Fabulous"*.

An officer came to get me processed through and took me to my designated cell for the night. Not realising this was only for the night, or knowing anything about prison life, I just went with it. *"Not as if I had any other choice"*. They housed me with two other girls who were visibly on class A drugs (Crack and heroin), but I didn't care; and they were pleasant. I settled down for the night and remembered thinking how much better this is in comparison to the police station. The beds were comfortable, and I remember being hungry and asking the officer if they had anything I could eat. He bought me a ham sandwich; I was happy, then I went to sleep. In the morning, the nurse came to the door hatch and administered medication to each of us. I was confused as I didn't take medication, yet she gave them to me, assuming I did. I took them and once she left, I just held them in my hand and said to the other girls, "what do I do with these? I don't take meds." They both simultaneously said "I'll have them" so I handed them over, they shared them between them then started to argue over which ones they wanted because the blue one seemed to be better than the others. I just laughed to myself and shrugged my shoulders, thinking that's between you two. An hour passed, and an officer came to collect me, saying, "You're being moved now." As we started to walk through the prison through gate after gate, it was then I realised, "ok, this is the *real* prison." It was a huge building with metal gates, bars and rows and rows of wings. They took me to my designated wing, based on my status: 'remand prisoner'. I had a visit, so she said, "I'll take you to your cell, leave your belongings, then I'll take you to the visiting hall." She opened the cell, and my new cellmate stood there. She was a large woman, and I noticed the cell was tiny. It was a single cell converted into a double and was no bigger than three by four meters in dimension. I said, "hi" to the woman who was in there, left my stuff and then went to my visit. The whole time I was on edge as I did not know what my fate was going to be once I returned.

Walking in the visiting room, I saw my mum and my auntie. My mum was completely beside herself and ran over with worry. I reassured her, "Don't worry, mum, I'm fine. Everything will be ok." Due to my circumstances before arriving, the controlling abuse I was enduring, I was *actually* ok. I felt safer and freer being in prison than I had for a long time. I was able to put on a strong face, as I always did, and gave my mum the reassurance she needed to make sure she was ok. I cut my visit short as I could not settle, and had an overwhelming feeling my new cellmate was going to steal the little belongings I had. When I got back, she was actually really nice. We spoke a lot over the next month as cellmates. She told me how she was on a charge for smuggling drugs, and she had a huge scar on her stomach where they had to cut the drugs out of her. You would never imagine someone so nice and well-presented would be going through these circumstances. However, this was a recurring pattern throughout my time in prison. Everyone had a different story, and many looked just like an auntie or a grandmother; yet they were all here with some horrific crimes accused against them. It made me realise you really cannot judge a book by its cover, yet also how significant an individual's circumstances and associations can be a main factor in the outcome of their life. As much as I found prison to be a release from the awful situation I was in before arriving, I struggled a lot with the day-to-day routines. The twenty-three hours of lock-up time every day, I found myself standing behind the door waiting anxiously for it to be opened - just to get more space and a change of atmosphere from this tiny cell. I'd gone for bail three times and was denied, which even my solicitors could not understand. I was a victim with a clean record. How could this be? I started to realise all hope had disappeared, and I needed to get accustomed to being there until I got my chance in court to prove my innocence. As unbelievable as it sounds, my abuser still had control over me while I was in prison. He didn't want me to get bail because he would lose control of my family. His mum would put him on a three-way call, and he would tell me what I had to do. I was not allowed to get bail and go and stay with my family. He would write me letters every day declaring his love for me and apologising, "in a perfect narcissistic fashion".

My long-awaited time for redemption arrived eight months later on remand. I had two days until my ten-week trial would start. Looking back now, I understand how the subconscious mind works, and I recall on the surface not feeling many emotions, yet it was something I was accustomed to, suppressing my conscious thoughts to protect myself from my reality. However, my physical body would react in different ways, which were out of my control. I had insomnia waiting for the trial to begin. The day had arrived, and I packed all my belongings and was awoken at 6 am to get on the bus heading for Crown Court in Nottingham. While I was waiting in the holding cell, another lady was there waiting to go to the same court. She looked very well-to-do in her appearance, wearing a tweed jacket and posh shoes. She was also well spoken, so I asked her what she had done. She told me she was on trial for murdering her husband. "shocking" Here I am, a victim of domestic violence being accused of crimes I never committed, yet facing the same fate as a murderer. "wow". We got on the high-security bus and arrived at court an hour and a half later. The press was waiting at the entrance and holding their cameras up to the bus windows, trying to capture a shot of the woman inside.

I was ushered in and placed in a holding cell beneath the courts. My time had come. They collected me, handcuffed me and into the courtroom I went. I stood in the dock with *him*, the person responsible for my nightmare, yet "he loves me. It isn't his fault", my delusional, weak, victimised mind told me. The court proceeded, and I was taken back to my cell. I remember getting impatient and ringing the intercom to ask where the bus was. I wanted to go back to prison. It was then that my solicitor came to see me. She stated the judge had offered me a plea bargain: drop one charge and lower another. She asked me what I wanted to do. I was completely out of my depth and had no understanding of the basic procedures, so it was absolutely pointless to expect me to answer with an adequate response. So, I asked her, "What do you think?" I asked her to make the decision. She said, "I'll go and tell the judge you accept the plea bargain," and off she went. Around thirty minutes passed, and an officer came to collect me. I was uncuffed, had my belongings handed to me and then a door opened. There I was, standing on the street, with my parents waiting for me. I could not believe it! I was free! "Wishful thinking, Sarah" Little did I know, my new sentence was just beginning. I was shipped to London to stay with my abusive boyfriend's mum as he started his nine-year sentence. And of course I went. "Stupid, weak little girl".

Fast forward three and a half years, and my mind and body had given up on me. My mental state had begun to decline, and at twenty-four years of age, I had a mental breakdown. I had to be rushed to get emergency medical assistance, "I lost my mind". Humans are not made to be suppressed, controlled, or locked in a cage. Even though I was out of prison, I was still held captive. I was still having every aspect and movement of my life controlled by the same person who was responsible for everything I had been through and was going through. "How is that love?".

A few days later, I packed all my stuff and arranged to collect a rental car. I had secured a place in a woman's refuge in Lincolnshire., I was done. I had nothing left to give. I sat in my room in silence for two days, trying to find the strength to leave and rationalise everything going on in my mind. The day had arrived when he called me in the morning, and I said, "I don't want to be with you anymore." He condescendingly laughed at me, as if he was thinking, "yeah, whatever. You can't, or won't, leave me". I hung up the phone. I told his mum, "I will be back soon to collect my belongings", then I left, got my car, collected my stuff and off I went. I cried uncontrollably, driving down the motorway from London to Lincoln. I had not told any of my family or the few friends I had made that I was leaving, so I could protect them. I had caused my mum enough over the years and couldn't bear the thought of her worrying, yet I needed to tell her so she could prepare herself if the worst should happen. I called her as I was getting closer to my destination. "Mum, I've left him. I'm ok and I'm going somewhere safe. Do not worry. I love you. I will be in contact as soon as I get settled." She replied, "ok, be careful. I love you." I could hear the fear in her voice.

A few months passed, and I'd spent that time getting used to being in control of my own life. I was trying to figure out my future. It was not easy. The damage was done, and being free from my past circumstances was not as exhilarating as I had initially anticipated. I'd had enough of hiding away in Lincoln and decided to move out of the women's refuge back to Nottingham to find myself again. I was still anxious, but he was still in prison, so I didn't care. I stayed with a friend and moved around a lot for the next year until I settled into a place. I let my friend move in with me as she was going through a difficult time and had nowhere to live. A year passed, and I met a guy who was kind to me. We remained friends for a year before becoming official, as I was just not ready to be with anyone, despite his consistent support and persistence to gain my love and trust. I finally gave in and realised he'd been good to me and that I had no reason to doubt him, to not give him a chance. I moved out of the house and left it to my friend.

I moved to Derbyshire for a fresh start and found out I was pregnant with my daughter. The timing was perfect. I spent the next nine months trying to prepare myself to become a mum. It was not something that came naturally to me. I had no maternal instincts and was always a tomboy. I also strongly believed I would never bring children into this evil world. However, I think because my daughter's father made me feel supported and safe, and I was older now, my body and mind were ready for this next chapter of my life. Things were going well in my life for once. I gave birth in October 2012 to my eight-pound beautiful bundle of joy and settled into motherhood. It was really difficult, yet I did not give up. I always tried my best to be a great mother, despite the difficulties we faced. No matter what, I always had an overwhelming feeling of worry knowing my ex was to be released at some point. I had heard stories that he'd lost his mind in prison and his behaviour had become even crazier and erratic than before. Just like I thought that day would come, and it did. I was at my mother's house with my daughter and heard a knock on the door. I was petrified and apprehensive to answer. I found the courage and opened the door. Two undercover police officers identified themselves and proceeded to tell me, "Sarah, he is out." I burst out crying, and I couldn't breathe. "What do you mean?" I asked. They told me, "He has finished his sentence. He's been released, and he has no conditions on him. He's moved back to Nottingham." My worst fear had become reality. I asked them, "How is this possible after everything he's done?" Then I said, "You lot stitched me up. I went to prison, and I never did anything!" They said, "We know you didn't, Sarah." I responded with, "Thanks! Now, fuck off!" I closed the door and called my partner. I explained what had happened and that I was worried my abuser would see me driving. "I'm afraid he'll see me with our child and hurt us, " my partner said, "try not to worry. Everything will be ok. There's no way on this planet I will let him hurt either of you." That gave me some reassurance, yet didn't take away the worry I carried deep in my soul.

Around three weeks passed, and I got home to lots of messages and missed calls. "he's dead" "What? Dead how?" I wasn't sure how I felt. I wasn't sure if I was in shock or not. There were no emotions. As the days passed, I realised the only emotion I felt was relief. Relief, he was gone. What can I say? As I've always said, "you can't be an evil person in this world and think God's going to allow you to live a good life." I guess I was right. That was his fate, and God knows he deserved it. "RIP" or "NOT".

Around a year after my abuser's death, unfortunately for my family, me, and my daughter's father parted ways. The last year of our relationship, he struggled with substance abuse and mental health issues. I had to make a choice: my daughter and me, or him. So, I left. My past experiences, no matter how much they broke me, also gave me a strength no one could ever take away from me. A strength that meant I would never allow myself to be made to feel the way that "horrible, evil piece of shit did." Never again in my life. I settled into being a single parent. It wasn't much difference, to be honest, as my daughter's father was not around much from the start, so I just got on with it. I had no choice; this little innocent girl had only me to protect her, love her and have someone to look up to. Despite all the difficulties I put my mum through, she always stood by me in the background, and she helped so much with my daughter that I would not have been able to cope, and for that, I am forever grateful.

I chose not to let my past define my future, and not to let the unfortunate events that had occurred break my spirit. I wasn't going to allow others' actions to force me to become what they tried to make me be. I blocked everything out, and used the new day God gives me to look forward, not backwards. I had to be strong, try to do and be a better person every single day. It's funny because I remember this defining moment as if it were yesterday. I remember where I was when I had this defining, unrealistic, significant idea of how I'm going to change my life around. I was driving past the University of Derby, a huge copper building in the city, saying to myself," Sarah, what do you want? You need to put yourself first." That was the first time, at twenty-nine years of age, I had ever asked myself that question. I always put everyone else first because I believed I didn't matter. Ironically, that building is where I graduated with my MSc degree in 2022. Everything, slowly but surely, began to change. I put myself first, and at twenty-nine, I took myself to adult college to gain my first ever qualification: a Diploma in Adult Social Care. I then applied and got accepted into the University of Derby onto a foundation degree which consisted of six subjects: A-level law, psychology, sociology, maths, English and study skills. I excelled in all subjects and passed everything, earning an automatic acceptance into my undergraduate degree in Forensic Psychology with a 2:2. I continued to get accepted into my Master's degree, earning a merit and a distinction in my dissertation.

I will be forever grateful for the opportunities the University of Derby gave me. Academia not only allowed me to learn my chosen subjects, but for the first time in my life, it gave me confidence, self-esteem, and self-belief, things I had never possessed. With everything I have achieved, I strongly believe that if I am capable of my achievements, despite the odds against me, and the difficulties I have faced in my life, YOU - whoever you are and whatever you're going through - are also capable and worthy of a better life. I also know real love is truly possible to find - and I'm grateful every day that I found it.

I hope reading my story can, and will, inspire you to carry hope in your heart no matter how dark your life feels. I pray you find confidence and courage. Remember, no matter how small that little bit of strength you have left is, with courage, hope and determination, you can build a new life. Step by step, little by little, and day by day, your strength will grow.

Trust me. I know.

Love Sarah x

# Women I'm Inspired By

*Debbie Tyler (Mum)*
My mother, Debbie Tyler, has been a defining influence throughout my life. Her resilience and unwavering work ethic have stood strong even in the face of personal hardship. Despite the challenges she has endured, she has consistently offered me steadfast support, stability, and

encouragement. Her determination not only shaped my values but also taught me what it truly means to persevere.

*Nana Dee Wright*
My Nana, Dee Wright, has been a pillar of strength and a source of unshakeable comfort. Her remarkable character, unconditional love, and constant presence have provided me with a genuine sense of belonging and emotional grounding. She instilled in me a deep appreciation for family, identity, and compassion - qualities that continue to guide me in every stage of my life.

# Reflections

## Ulrika Karlsson
## Sweden

Ulrika "Ullis" Karlsson is a Menopause and Stress Management Expert, Spiritual Teacher, and Mentor for Women walking the sacred fires of change. Known as The Sage and Keeper of Wisdom, she guides women to alchemize the "shitstorm" of menopause into soulful alignment , where radiance, pleasure, and purpose are reclaimed.

With more than 30+years of experience of guiding and supporting women, and through her grounded yet deeply spiritual work, Ulrika helps women transmute exhaustion, rejection, and overwhelm into embodied wisdom and freedom. She is the founder of Bloom Beyond Menopause Summit and holistic programs, author of several transformational books, and a global voice for women's awakening through midlife initiation
https://ulliskarlsson.com/
https://www.linkedin.com/in/ulrika-ullis-karlsson

# Owning My Ovaries, Owning My Energy

Congratulations on holding Owning My Ovaries in your hand! This means you have called her in, and that you, my friend, are ready for a change. Ready to own your ovaries.

I have been asked by my dear friend Dawn Bates, the author, publisher, and creator of this book, "Owning Our Ovaries", to write a chapter. And it really made me sit with it and contemplate - What does that even mean, to own my ovaries? For me, it simply means: Not just literally owning my ovaries merely on the physical anatomical plane, but owning my energy. To own and reclaim my power, my Heart and Crown chakra energy. To own my voice, and to share my truth and my story, her story.

One of my intentions with this story is to honour the Divine Feminine energy; it is a celebration of Life itself. All the challenges and hardships that mould us into the Goddesses that we are, but not always feel like experiencing, or are connected to. Yet, every change is Divinely guided by Source for our Souls' growth! This chapter is for you, and for me, to remember, to reclaim our voice and stand in our truth. To both descend into the Heart chakra and rise into the Crown chakra, to remember and embrace who we are on a Soul level.

For thousands of years, we have been unconsciously separated from the Feminine story, which has been distorted, disconnected, ridiculed, rewritten, reshaped, silenced - HER-story hidden inside, suppressed beneath HIS-story. Yet the time of remembering has come. The Feminine voice is no longer a whisper beneath the weight of old systems; she rises now, through each of us who dare to feel, to burn, to clear out the old and to become the new. The Divine Feminine is awakening, fiercely and unapologetically, to help us remember who we are on a Soul level and to reconnect us to our inner wisdom. This profound wisdom, which is intimately connected to both the wisdom of Gaia - the energies of the Root & Heart chakra - also the Crown chakra, and the Universal wisdom.

My name, Ulrika, means *Magnificent* in Swedish; a name once given to Swedish Queens. I didn't always feel magnificent. I have never, until quite recently, actually, felt like a Queen. This chapter is about my transition into the Crown energy, the Queen energy, and the Goddess archetype. Every challenge and hardship, transition, initiation, every loss, every insight, and every scar has guided me back to that inner throne: the archetype of the Queen and the Wise Woman that lives within each one of us. This is my story of how she was reawakened. Welcome <3

"To own my ovaries - is to wear my Crown, as the Diamond it is ..."

## And so, the Fire Begins

It was Christmas 2021. The world outside was trembling in fear - a planet caught and trapped in panic over a tiny crown-shaped virus. "Corona," they called it. Which, in Spanish, means *Crown*. The world as we knew it was spinning in fear, manipulation and control, masked faces, censorship, and silenced Hearts. And this "news" was broadcast on mainstream media twenty-four hours a day, seven days a week.

Long before Christmas 2021, I knew, as a Yogi with knowledge of ancient Yogic scripts, this was the global storm that had been mentioned for thousands of years. The Yogic Veda scripts have long shared about this big shift, this important transition that is here to awaken humanity from a deep unconscious slumber, one where old systems will crumble and fall apart. That all we know as familiar would fall, an immense opportunity for a global shift into higher states of consciousness. It would also act as a mirror of the inner shift, as old fear-based programmes rose to the surface in the individual and collective consciousness.

Yet deep within, another storm was unknowingly forming - my own. Humanity was being asked to connect deeper into our Hearts, awaken and ascend into the *Crown chakra*, to rise from old fear-based narratives into higher vision, with more clarity, and also more empathy and Love for ourselves and also for others. Instead, most people unconsciously choose fear and the narrative. I did not follow the fear or bring the narrative into my life, yet it was hard to avoid as it was everywhere. It was on TV, mainstream news, radio, family discussion; it was everywhere! I followed my Heart, my own truth and little did I know at the time that the cost of following my Heart and speaking my truth was coming with great costs at my own expense.

That Christmas, I went to my sister's house, grateful for family in uncertain times. I said, "Hi!" and hugged everyone, and finally, my brother-in-law, a quick hug, yet in that moment, a shiver ran through me, a deep inner knowing, I intuitively knew something was really off. And my intuition, unfortunately, was right. Within twenty-four hours, a rash appeared on my body: red, burning, itching and alive with fire. It turned out my brother-in-law had taken the "COVID-19 vaccine" just a couple of days before Christmas, and I unknowingly got something called "shedding" from the injection he had taken. I had refused to have the vaccines, choosing to follow my own intuition and inner guidance, remembering the ancient scripts - but it seemed like I got it anyway, out of nowhere, through this hug.

Looking back, it is mind-boggling that a little hug could have initiated all that fire, all that pain, and the challenges that became my reality for five and a half months, and how it took me into a deep transition on multiple, multidimensional levels.

Over the following days, the rash spread quickly, crawling up my arms toward my throat and all the way down to my ankles. Every morning, new areas of my body were invaded by new, inflamed, burning rashes. The skin was aggressively red, it blistered, cracked, and itched, and the pain was so intense. It felt as though I were burning alive at the stake - like the witch I have been in many lifetimes, and still am. It was like a combination of old cellular memories and the shedding from the injection, something many believe to be a ridiculous notion... until they experience it.

Twenty-four seven, the rash itched. It seared. It was alive, it burned and screamed.
And so did I. Night after night, I lay awake; skin aflame, Soul unravelling, feeling the heat and the pain of every woman before me who had been judged, silenced, burned, banished, and called "witch." The memory wasn't only mine. I truly felt it was *ours*. Each blister whispered the names of women who had been erased from history, their wisdom buried beneath the ashes of patriarchy. Now, that buried wisdom was trying to be rebirthed through me. Through my body. Through my skin. I wanted to run, to escape. I wanted to disappear. I wanted to die. Instead, I was forced to stay - inside the fire, inside my body, and inside of pain. Five and a half months. No sleep. No rest. Just fire and raw, burning pain.

During this process, my partner and I were living in a small mobile home in another city, far away from friends and family. He left early for work, and I was left alone with my skin, my pain, my rashes, my screams, and the silence. Each morning, I followed my fragile thread of sanity - my ritual. I allowed my body to show me the way, what it needed. I danced, moved, and shook. I cried, I breathed. Every day, I laid down multiple times in the ice-cold snow to cool off and soothe my aching, burning, raw skin. All day, I wore a robe, even on my walks with Daisy (my dog, healer, and best friend), as I could not wear clothes due to the pain and rawness of my skin. I moved through pain until movement itself became prayer. Yoga, breathwork, meditation - these were my anchors in a burning hell that wanted to consume me. But some mornings, even those anchors slipped through my fingers. The despair came like waves, hissing, "*Just give up. Let go. You are not wanted. What's the point?*"

Society had cast me out due to my different opinions and perspectives. I had lost my work, every contract, every client. My collaborations, income, and my visibility - all gone. Even my social media accounts were silenced, closed, censored, shut down. I had been labelled "different," "reckless", and "wrong." I, who had spent decades guiding others into healing and wholeness, was now the outcast - standing alone while the world pointed its fingers, betrayed me, and turned away.

Fear had made everyone forget who they were. Fear created separation and hatred.
I felt betrayed, rejected, and abandoned. The disappointment I felt when a Swedish Yoga travel company I'd co-created retreats with for over a decade quietly ended our collaboration. No explanation, just silence, rejection and creating a distance - the kind of silence that echoes louder than words.

And so, I lived in "exile" - burned from the inside, burned from the outside.

The rash was not just on my skin; it was in my Soul. I felt branded. Branded as the witch, the heretic, the one who would not bow. Each night, as the fire within me raged, I remembered lifetimes where women like me had burned - for knowing too much, for speaking too clearly and standing up for their truths, for refusing to forget the ancient ways. It was as if every cell in my being was screaming with the memory of those flames. And yet, through the tears, there was a faint voice, "*Stay in your truth, Ulrika. Don't give in. Don't give up.*"

At night, I didn't sleep. My sheets were covered in flakes of skin. Each morning, it looked as if I had shed a former self, like a snake shedding its skin. Pain replaced rest, distress replaced ease and despair replaced appetite. My body was an inferno, a living hell to be in, and I had nowhere to hide, nowhere to go. I thought I was losing my mind.

As the days, on repeat, turned into weeks and months, the sensation of being burned alive came and went. With no sleep, I became depressed. I wondered how I would survive the excruciating pain. Every day, I had thoughts that I no longer wanted to live.

*How do I endure?*
*How can I live through the burning pain?*
*How can I stand to live in this society, where I am treated as an outcast, just because I did not want to take the so-called "COVID-19 vaccine"?*

My family didn't understand or support my choice, or try to acknowledge my truth of why I did not want to take the "vax". Friends turned away. People's ugliest unconscious sides were displayed everywhere. Projections, hatred, fear, disconnection, exclusion, and separation that even went through family lineages, within families. People who were once my friends, my clients, created the separation - we versus them. Or rather, the illusion of separation. There were the good ones who did what they were told by society, media, governments, the mainstream narrative, versus the conspiracy theorists, the irresponsible tinfoil hats with other narratives, other truths.

We know that a circle has three hundred and sixty degrees, yet only one degree of the circle was displayed by mainstream media, and across all Societies around the world. There was no opposition. No debate. No discussion. Just one degree, one narrative that was allowed to be visible. Everyone who had a different narrative was silenced. There was so much fear, hatred, and separation in the individual *and* the collective consciousness all over the world, and it was the first time in my life, in this lifetime, that I found myself in the midst of all the fear-based projections.

Bullied. Belittled. Ridiculed. Silenced. Censored. Hated. Manipulated. Excluded. Threatened.

My economic lifeline, my income, was taken from me, shut down. Society labelled me "tinfoil hat" - delusional, irresponsible, a heretic. I felt the same old archetypal wounds of the Medicine woman who knows too much, and that needs to be silenced, one way or another.

As my body burned, the planet burned with it. Humanity was having its own rash - inflamed, red, raw. Fear and division spread faster than any physical contagion. The virus was not only in the lungs; it was in the Hearts of people.

Corona - the Crown.

*Could it be that this whole collective ordeal actually was a Crown initiation? A purification of the seventh chakra, humanity's collective connection to Source, to wisdom, to divine consciousness?*

This was, and still is, by belief, my truth.

The world was afraid of the virus, of death, but what was really dying was illusion. Old structures, old power systems, old ways of control - all crumbling. We were all being asked to step into sovereignty, to remember our Divine authority. But instead of rising into our Crowns, most fell into the fears and ran away from the fire.

My own body was mirroring this collective alchemy. My skin, my largest organ, was purging centuries of fear, suppression, and trauma - the witch wound, the healer wound, the mother wound. Every flake of skin that fell away carried a memory of being silenced, censored, burned, and cast out.

And yet, beneath the ashes, something shimmered. I began to see 11:11 on clocks, 22:22 on receipts, and Sacred geometry appearing in the smallest of coincidences. The universe was whispering: *You are not alone.*

From my ankles to my neck, the burning rashes became my teacher. They forced me to completely stop, to surrender, to face and to move through the fire. To face my fears. The rashes made me stay with the pain. To heal wounds, express unexpressed emotions, and transmute traumas to clear out old Karmic cords stored as cellular memories. To move through hell and to rise in consciousness, shifting from denser, lower vibrational darkness - and eventually into more, higher vibrational light.

# Punishment

### *"Burn baby burn"*

Each night, as the burning intensified, I would whisper to the darkness, *"Why am I being punished? What have I done to deserve this but to speak my truth? Why am I not allowed to speak my truth in a society that claims to have freedom of speech?"*

The answers eluded me, and only silence answered - until silence itself became both the answer and presence. The human part of me resisted the fire in my skin, fought, cried, begged, and prayed for relief. I longed to belong, to be included in society. And at the same time, something deeper within me observed the burning. I began to sense that this was more than a physical reaction. The fire was an alchemy of some sort. Even if I could not logically know or understand why, I felt it was a transition that I would either give in to and die, or "die and rise", being rebirthed into someone new.

Now, I realise that just as carbon becomes a diamond under massive heat and pressure for a long time, I was also being refined, even though I did not know it at the time. Every old belief, every memory of persecution, every unhealed wound rose to the surface to literally be burned away and cleared out.

There are moments in a woman's life when her body becomes a temple of truth - not gentle, not polite, not like a whisper - but raw, burning, roaring and unapologetically alive. Menopause was that temple of truth for me. It didn't arrive with grace or ceremony. Not even expected. It came blazing through my skin. It came as fire, through the fire. It came as hell on earth.

As if the physical, mental, and emotional agony, pain, and the excessive heat and burning sensations all over my body were not enough, the fire triggered me into Menopause. Menopause, the great transition from the fertility of the body to the fertility of the Soul. However, it certainly did not feel like a Sacred transition at the time. My hormones shifted, my cycles stopped, my energy withdrew inward, and a new kind of hell emerged.

I experienced so much brain fog, exhaustion, and total absence of sleep. Now, when I look back, I realise I wasn't punished; I was being redirected into a whole new level of Sacredness. As the container that was my body no longer "leaked energy, as in moon blood," and with the energy container intact, it enabled me to rise into the Crown chakra. My system was recalibrating, asking me to embody a new vibration. In those five and a half months, I unconsciously entered what Mystics call *the Dark Night of the Soul*. To me, it was like purgatory, like hell. Whatever name we give it, it is the Sacred space between who we were and who we are BEcomING. A Sacred Initiation. We become what our Souls have chosen us to be long before we even incarnate into physical bodies here on planet Earth.

During these five and a half months, I went to doctors to see what was wrong with me. They called the inflamed and infected rashes "stress" or "reaction." They wanted me to take cortisone creams and painkillers, which I refused. What doctors called stress and reaction actually later turned out to be a *rebirth*.

There were days when I didn't want to stay in my body. When I fantasised about ending the pain, ending my life and the story altogether. When even my spiritual tools felt hollow, and the only thing left was breath. In those moments, I understood what it means to die before you die. And perhaps that's what Menopause truly is - A Sacred Death? And a Sacred Rebirth at the same time. The death of roles, expectations, of being the good girl, the caregiver, the one who keeps it all together, all the illusions, all the stories told.

> "Menopause doesn't destroy you. She dismantles what is false.
> She strips you naked so that only truth remains."

## The Realisation

One morning, after yet another sleepless night, I caught my reflection in the mirror. My skin was still burning red and inflamed, my eyes were tired, yet there was a spark behind the exhaustion; I saw some light. It was faint, yes, but at least there was some light. There was light where there had been fire. That was the moment I knew I had crossed some kind of threshold.

Within me, I sensed more than heard a whisper:
"You are not being punished. You are being purified. You are not rejected; you are being redirected. All is well. You are doing so well. New things await you at the end of this tunnel. You are nearly there..."

As lightning from a clear sky, I just knew. The rashes, the isolation, the loss, the pain and all the struggle - all of it was my body's way of releasing what no longer matched the vibration of my emerging self, the one I was BEcomING. My body wasn't betraying me. It was *initiating* me. The chaos I experienced was the language of transformation, the Sacred Feminine and the Sacred Masculine that burned away thousands of years of illusions and fear-based programs.
But God, it was brutal.

The shedding from the "vaxx", and being forced into Menopause, turned out not to be the end; it was a *transition and an alignment of body, mind and Soul with access and a deepened connection to my inner wisdom.*

When I finally surrendered, when I stopped resisting the pain and whispered, *"Okay, I surrender, let it all burn"*, - something changed. Eventually, the fire softened. It became light. The blisters healed, leaving scars that glowed like constellations - reminders of where I had been tempered. I no longer saw them as marks of suffering, but as symbols of resilience and initiation. This deep process truly had become a transition into owning my truth, my power, and my story. Owning My Ovaries. Not only as anatomy, but as energetic portals. Ovaries, the seat of creation, intuition, love, and power - my inner alchemist. Through the fire, I discovered that the ovaries aren't just biological organs - they are Sacred cauldrons. When we stop producing eggs, we begin to deepen the connection to our inner wisdom. When our blood stops flowing outward, our energy turns inward and upward, travelling into the Crown chakra, and to higher states of consciousness.

*Menopause is not an ending. It is ascension. It is the body's own wise alchemy - a shift from fertile woman to fertile wisdom keeper. We've been taught to fear this transition, to medicate it, to hide it, to feel shame around it; But what if it's actually the initiation the world needs us to remember?*

I was shedding not just skin, but lifetimes, programmes, traumas, lies and illusions.
Every hot flash became a prayer.
Every tear, like a baptism.
And slowly, I began to feel her - the powerful and wise Queen within. Not a monarch of power over others, but a sovereign of her own energy. She emerged from the ashes, Crown illuminated not by gold but by light from facing life's challenges, ups and downs.

Owning my ovaries was never just physical; it was about remembering my Divinity. Reclaiming my right to create, to feel, to lead from within. It was about standing in my power, in my voice and truth - unapologetically. To own my "shit", to own my story. The world burned, and I burned with it, but in that shared inferno, something Sacred was rebirthed. The woman who walked into that fire was small, afraid, excluded, still trying to adapt to someone else's world. The woman who emerged was carved by flame - fierce, crystalline, and unapologetically sovereign.

"The more unconscious traumas we carry, the more challenges we face in the Sacred fires of Menopause, as we let go of the old to rise into the new."

## The Rebirth: The Diamond Phase

There is a point in every initiation where the fire no longer burns - it begins to illuminate. But to reach that light, you must walk through every layer of darkness that once defined you. For me, that darkness was not metaphorical; it was physical, emotional, mental, spiritual, and it lived in my skin.

Sometimes the body becomes the altar. Sometimes the offering is everything you thought you were.
Those rashes - angry, raw, weeping - became the Sacred script of my Soul. They told the story of the witch who had been burned. The healer who had been silenced.

The woman who had once dimmed her light to belong.
It was no coincidence that this all happened as I crossed into Menopause.
Because Menopause is a *threshold*.

> "Menopause is the Soul's initiation from doing to being, from fertility of the womb to fertility of wisdom."

## The Heart and the Thymus: The Forgotten Gateway

As the fire continued, something else began to awaken with a tender ache behind my breastbone: The thymus gland. A small, butterfly-like organ that sits above the Heart, the seat of the higher Heart chakra. It's where compassion meets courage, where self-love transforms into service. Most of us never feel it. But in transformation, the thymus comes alive. When I placed my hand there, between my breasts, I could feel the pulse of something ancient, like a spark of my Divine essence flickering back to life. This was like a *bridge* between the human and the Divine, between the suffering and the Sacred. The thymus is also where immunity lives, not just the physical immune system, but the energetic immunity to fear, shame, and separation.
It's the organ that reminds us: *"You are safe to be who you truly are."*

As my skin burned, my Heart burned too.
It was grief.
It was love.
It was lifetimes and timelines collapsing into one heartbeat.

> "And beneath that pain, I found compassion, first for myself, then for every woman who had ever been consumed by the flames, internally and externally."

# The Path of the Heart and Crown

When the Heart opens, forgiveness also starts to flow. Forgiveness for the body that changed, for the people who didn't understand, for the years you abandoned your own needs to keep others comfortable.
The thymus expands when we speak our truth. When we breathe with love instead of fear. When we remember that our softness is strength. From the Heart, the energy rises to the Crown, where the Queen waits, luminous, grounded, wise. The Heart and the Crown chakras are the seat of the Sage, the Healer, the Alchemist. It's where the noise quiets, and the Soul speaks. When these two centers align - Heart and Crown - we embody *sovereign grace*.

The Queen doesn't demand. She emanates.
She creates not from scarcity, but from Sacredness.
That is the woman I became through my own fire. That is the woman waiting within every Menopausal body - radiant, horny for life, humming with Divine intelligence.

That's the secret no one tells you about Menopause: it's not just hormonal, emotional, physical, and mental; it is all of that and more. It's alchemical.
The oestrogen, progesterone, and testosterone are just messengers, responding to the deeper calling of the Soul.

> "When one fertile cycle ends, another begins - the hormones of reproduction give way to the hormones of awakening. It is an ascension process, connecting all chakras, especially the energy of Love and compassion in the Heart chakra, merging with the Crown chakra, and the access to Universal Love."

# The Crown Chakra: The Queen's Ascension

As my body burned, another fire rose, one of light, of awareness and consciousness - not heat. It was subtle at first, a tingling, a spaciousness, an expansion beyond thought, beyond understanding. This was the Crown Chakra, the *Sahasrara*, the thousand-petaled lotus. It's the portal to Divine wisdom, the seat of our connection to the cosmos.

During Menopause, as the reproductive hormones quieten down, the body's energy naturally begins to move upward, to ascend into and energetically ignite the Crown chakra. This is why so many women in Menopause experience bursts of intuition, hot flashes, vivid dreams, spiritual awakening, or a sudden desire for solitude.

Menopause is not a breakdown. It's a *breakthrough*.

The Crown asks us to release control, to trust and to surrender to something larger. But surrender is terrifying when you've built your whole life around holding everything together.

> "For me, surrender came through exhaustion. And through fire.
> And the Universe replied, not with words, but with stillness and presence."

## The Archetypes Awaken

As I began to integrate this initiation, I could feel the archetypes stirring; those ancient energies that live within all women and men as we expand our consciousness.
The Sage whispered, *"You are the keeper of wisdom now. You don't need to seek. You remember that all is within."*
The Healer murmured, *"Your path is Sacred proof that energy transforms."*
The Alchemist smiled, *"Turn this pain into your medicine. Share it with the world."*
The Queen stood tall, not with power over others, but in her truth and with true power *from within*. Her crown wasn't jewelled, it was made of light.

Each archetype was awakened by the blazing fire. Menopause, I further realised, is not a loss of identity. It is the revelation of who you have always been.

The more trauma from this, and other lifetimes that are stored in our bodies, stored in our ovaries, the more the symptoms need to "burn away", the more challenging the Sacred transition of Menopause might be.

"When the ovaries quiet, the womb of creation doesn't die, the energy moves upward, into the Heart and the Crown. You connect to higher states of consciousness and get more access to the light within you. This is the hidden meaning of Menopause. It is the initiation into embodied wisdom. It is when the woman becomes her own oracle, the keeper of wisdom."

## The Diamond Emerges

The diamond phase is not gentle. It's forged in pressure, in fire, in surrender, in absolute trust. But once the transformation occurs, something extraordinary happens. The energy that once burned you begins to radiate through you. When carbon becomes diamond, it doesn't lose its essence; it becomes clearer, stronger, more precious, and radiant. That is what Menopause did for me. My skin eventually healed. My light came back, softer, wiser, truer. And through the ashes of everything I had lost, my career, my job, my clients, assignments, my connections, my sense of belonging, I found something far more precious: Myself.

> "Menopause was not my ending - It was my coronation."

And that is what I now share with women; that beneath, beyond, the hot flashes and brain fog, beneath the sleepless nights and forgotten words, there is a Sacred invitation: To shed skin. To awaken. To remember. To bloom beyond.

## The Integration: Blooming Beyond

Every initiation carries its medicine, a calling. Mine was fire. Yours may come in another form: fatigue, a dis-ease, or a deep, indescribable ache, a transition of sorts. Menopause has a thousand faces, and yet one purpose: To call us home. For months, I lived inside the burning, shedding, awakening - until the woman I had been could no longer exist. From that fire, something new emerged: not the Ulrika who once served from depletion and duty, but the Magnificent woman who creates from sovereignty, from Soul, from walking through the fire.

I knew I had to share and harness the power of all I had learnt in life, and through this powerfully potent experience of 'shedding' from the "vaxx" my brother-in-law had taken. It was that moment Bloom Beyond Menopause was born, even though I did not realise it at the time. Not only was Bloom Beyond Menopause a deeply transformative, tailor-made programme and a Summit to serve other women in Menopause, but it was a pulse, a Sacred space for women who are done surviving and ready to *bloom and rise.*

The Healing Journey

When I finally surrendered to this inner knowing, real healing began. I stopped fighting the fire and started listening to it. Each itch became a message and a challenge to surrender to it. Each sleepless night, a meditation, a test of resilience and a proof of how much I could handle, navigate through.

I returned to my mat and deepened my practice in my own uniquely designed Yoga for Hormones, refining it into Yoga for Menopause. I developed sequences that open and nourish the ovaries, adrenals, and thyroid, the OAT axis that anchors Feminine vitality, each gland a Sacred portal. This helped me tremendously. On my healing journey, I used frequency medicine, alchemy, and simply allowed Life to come and go. To move through this was challenging on so many levels, as Trust, Acceptance, and Patience have never been easy for me.

A big shift for me was also when I accepted one friend's gentle reminder: *"You have already burned away the old. It's safe to soothe what remains. What you have cleared out is gone, and won't come back. Allow yourself to get the ease your body needs so you can continue to heal."*

So, after five and a half months of raw skin, a burning itch from hell and endless sleepless nights, I finally used the cortisone cream all over my body, which doctors had suggested for months. I surrendered and released my resistance to mainstream medicines. Within days, the flames quieted. My body exhaled. Scars remained, but they were maps of transformation, not shame, defeat, or failure.

My skin burned because I was literally shedding the old frequency of who I used to be. I realised that the body is not separate from Spirit - it's the messenger and the container. And that the rashes and the fire were my body screaming, *"It's time to rise."*

The woman who emerged from that fire was not the same woman who had entered it. I was lighter, clearer, stronger. I felt grateful for coming back to Life and could feel my ovaries as centres of creative power again, pulsing with quiet intelligence and embodied wisdom.

## The Teaching

Every woman and man carries this potential within to transmute pain, struggle, and shift into higher states of consciousness, gain access to more light, more wisdom. Through the pressure to become a diamond.

As I write this, doctors are talking about Menopause on Swedish TV, and admitting how little they truly know about it, and that the treatments for it here in Sweden are so old-fashioned and outdated. Menopause, in our modern societies, have been distorted and turned into something ugly and shameful, where it is being proven by women the world over to be a Sacred transition, a shift in consciousness... if women allow themselves to surrender to it, learn from it and transform through it.

In ancient traditions, and from the Yogic perspectives, Menopause is seen as entering the Crown energy, connecting to the Queen/Goddess archetype. Throughout the ages, the elder and the wise, the woman others turn to for advice, support, healing, and ancient wisdom shared and passed on from generation to generation, over the bonfires. Women today are losing this connection, especially in the Western world, where ageing is being fought against and our elders are dismissed and abandoned in care homes, left to die whilst their families move on without them. We are losing our connection to ancient wisdom as women, as society and humanity as a whole. And we need to return to ourselves, to one another, to our higher callings of BEing.

When the ovaries slow their physical production, they hand their energetic codes to the adrenals and thyroid, forming a new trinity of wisdom. When balanced, this OAT axis sustains a woman's light for the second half of life. When neglected, it mirrors the collective exhaustion of a world that has forgotten how to honour the Feminine.

Through the fire, I learned that the body's symptoms are not enemies. They are invitations to listen. The hot flash is the body's way of burning through unexpressed emotions and old unresolved trauma. The brain fog invites stillness. The sleepless nights whisper: *"Wake up; something within you wants to be born."*

## The Rebirth

To own my ovaries, for me, means to own my creative power, my fire, my voice, my truth, and my story; to reclaim my energy and deepen my connection to the wisdom that resides within. To own my ovaries means to remember that every ending is also an initiation into deeper sovereignty. To own my ovaries is a calling and a possibility to heal and to rewrite my story, as in HER story.
This is not just my story. It is our story, the story of women remembering who we are, here to rewrite the narrative from survival and fear-based programs into Sacred embodiment. It is a story of reclamation and rebirth.

When we reclaim our ovaries, we reclaim the Sacred seat of creation. When we heal the heart, we return to compassion. When we activate the Crown, we remember who we truly are - Divine consciousness in human form. The word *Corona* means *Crown*. The world's Crown initiation mirrored my own. And through that fire, both I and humanity were asked the same question: Will you rise in fear, or in love?

I chose love.

*Owning My Ovaries is not just a story. It's a map.* A map back to the sacred feminine that lives within every woman. A reminder that menopause is not a disease to fix, but a doorway to your Divinity. Through the Heart, through the Crown, through the fire, we rise. We remember. We reign.

### *From Fire to Flowering*

When I look back on those long, burning nights, I can see now that every flame was holy. The pain that once felt unbearable became the forge that shaped me into who I am today. What I lost were the layers that had kept me small, feeling excluded and afraid of being different.

What remained was the truth. My truth. Perhaps you have another truth, and that is ok.

I know what it feels like to be cast out, to be misunderstood, to lose work, friends, clients, reputation, money, and belonging because I dared to listen to my own body, my own wisdom. But I also know what it feels like to rise again - freer, fiercer, and more radiant than ever before.

Menopause is not a medical failure or hormonal curse; it is a Sacred initiation. It asks us to lay down the armour we've carried for decades, lifetimes even, and remember who we are beneath it all.

When we burn away the "shoulds," the conditioning, the unresolved traumas, and all external noise, what emerges is our true essence - raw, sensual, wise, creative. That essence is not something we must earn or learn; it has always been there, pulsing quietly beneath the surface, waiting for our permission to bloom. Creating the unique, tailor-made program for women ahead of/in the midst of, and past Menopause; *Bloom Beyond Menopause - How to Be Happy, Horny & Healthy, I knew with every cell of my body and magical spark of my soul that it was* not just a course. I created a Sacred journey, a reclamation for women who are ready to rise. Ready to bloom.

## Bloom Beyond Menopause: How to be Happy, Horny, and Healthy

After my burning experience, I burned in another way. This burning was a desire and a calling to serve other women who are struggling with, and during, Menopause. My lesson, my teaching, my transition also became my calling.

The calling was to work together with women for six months, to guide women through a path that mirrored my own alchemy, but that would be their own sovereign journey. With my journey, I remembered, released, reclaimed, rose up, radiated, and bloomed. I knew that each month I had suffered had been significant. There are no coincidences or mistakes in nature. Five and a half months of burning led to a six-month journey for my new clients, ones who are soul and frequency aligned. And we'd begin by reclaiming the story of Menopause as a Sacred transition, not a decline. I would encourage and guide women to learn to listen to their body's whispers instead of fearing its changes.

Returning to my mat through these dark months, I knew I had created a uniquely designed *Yoga for Menopause*. All the breathwork, energy rituals, and clearing cellular memories - emotional, ancestral, and energetic residue - I did when my body burned to renew would become the practices I would share with my new community. The reclaiming of my soul and Queen within has allowed me to rediscover the true meaning of my creative and sexual energy, and as women, we need to explore how to awaken desire from within through meditation, movement, and sacred embodiment. Practices which are not always easy for so many women.

Activating my Heart and Crown chakras, expanding my thymus energy, and integrating higher frequencies of self-trust and love for self also became a pillar of my new programme, how could it not with all I'd been through? When I finally surrendered, I started to radiate through learning how to live as the Queen, my namesake. BEcomING the Healer, the Alchemist was the next natural step, helping women to balance in hormones, energy, and purpose, allowing themselves to bloom. The blooming, I knew, was the final phase bringing everything together for happiness, health, and vitality that flows from alignment, not effort. No hustle, no pushing, simply receiving from being at peace and accepting ourselves; blooming beyond limitation, beyond fear, beyond Menopause itself.

Why This Work Matters

I had spent too many years asleep, and yet I was more awake than many. And what the world needs now more than ever is women who are awake; women who have transmuted their pain into presence, their cycles into wisdom, their "Shitstorm" into Soulful alignment. We are not here to fade quietly, to be shamed or to be discarded. We are here to reign gracefully. When a woman owns her ovaries, she owns her world. When she heals her thymus, she heals her Heart.

When she opens her Crown, she channels Divine intelligence into everything she touches. This is the Sacred Feminine Renaissance, and Menopause is the doorway.

My Invitation to You

If you are reading this and something inside of you whispers, "Yes... I feel it. I'm ready," then this is my invitation to you: Surrender. Allow yourself to feel, release and unravel. And if you feel called to, join me for Bloom Beyond Menopause: How to Be Happy, Horny, and Healthy, the transformational journey I birthed from my own surrendering. It is where science meets Spirit, where hormones meet holiness, and where your body becomes your teacher again.

I resisted my body, made her wrong for so many years, fell for the narratives of what beauty should be, rather than what it truly is. And together, we will rise through the fire, reconnect with the diamond wisdom within, and remember what it means to live, fully, fiercely, freely.
Because to not live fully, to live fiercely and with freedom, is no life at all. It is just an existence, one created by the programming and structures we have all grown up surrounded by. The systems and beliefs we have been forced to conform to. What I have forged through my fire is for you who want to alchemise the "shitstorm" of life, of living in a shackled society, and the journey of modern-day Menopause. We can alchemise these feelings of confusion, of being stuck, of feeling less than into clarity, freedom, and abundance with Soul alignment.

Because Menopause is not the end of my story, your story or the women who follow on from us.
It's the beginning of our sovereignty.
And our Crown, dear sister, dear Queen, is waiting for us to reclaim it.

## Reclaiming The Real Meaning of "Horny"

As I speak of reclaiming all that is ours, I also want to take the opportunity to reclaim the power of the word Horny. It is a word that, in our modern society, has been very distorted. We've been told it's about pleasing others, performing, or chasing validation. But the truth is far more Divine. Being horny is not just about sex; it's about *life force*. Being connected to your own life force. It's your creative current, your Shakti, your Sacred pulse that says, *I am alive*. It's the same energy that births galaxies, that fuels art, poetry, healing, and laughter.

When oestrogen and progesterone shift, so does that current - not to disappear, but to transform. In Menopause, our sensuality no longer lives for others - it turns inward, reconnecting us with our essence. We stop seeking approval and begin to radiate authenticity.
Horniness becomes holiness. Pleasure becomes presence. Our body becomes our temple again.

And during the revelation and creation process of In *Bloom Beyond Menopause: How to Be Happy, Horny, and Healthy*, I knew I had to help women remember this. Not by teaching them who to be, but by guiding them back to the truth of who they already are, who they have desired to become but pushed down to please others, and ultimately guiding them to the truth of who they are already becoming,

As I mentioned before, I did not feel safe during my time of resisting the "COVID-19 Vaccination", and it is vital for us as women to feel safe for us to flourish. Bloom Beyond Menopause needed to be a safe, for ALL of who women are. Their ideas, their beliefs, and their desires. Allowing the ideas and my intuition to flow, I knew the Sacred space where we came together as women would explore the intelligence of the body, the power of breath, the medicine of movement, and the art of surrender. I knew the women who felt called to this would laugh, cry, and reconnect to the life force that the world told us to suppress. We would be reclaiming the word 'horny' for ourselves. Because "horny" is not about performance - it's about power. Because "happy" is not about pretending - it's about presence. And "healthy" is not about perfection - it's about harmony.

I believe every woman deserves to live from this embodied truth - to walk through the world radiant, centred, and sovereign. If my story has touched you, let it remind you that you, too, are designed to heal. You, we, are wired for renewal, for expansion, for love. There is nothing wrong with us; we are simply being initiated into our next level of wisdom. Our body is not our enemy - it is our temple. Our menopause is not our ending - it is our coronation. And you, dear sister, are not too late - you are right on time. Welcome home to yourself, your radiance. Welcome home to your Crown.

HERstory Rising

Today, when I run my hands over my skin, even though the scars from the fire are healed, my body remembers. Menopause, like initiation, is not for the faint-hearted. It asks us to face our shadows, to sit in the fire, to release what no longer serves us. But it also offers the Crown, the radiant wisdom of knowing that we have *always* been whole.

And so, I share my story not as a tragedy, but as an offering, an alternative narrative to that one that is being presented in mainstream media.

To the woman reading this who feels alone in her night of burning - know this: You are not being punished. You are being purified. You are being redefined. You are being rebirthed - you are being remembered by your Soul.

To the one who feels lost - the path is not ahead, it is within. Own your ovaries. Own your power. Own your light. Let the ashes of your old identity nourish the soil of your rebirth. For you, too, are the Queen returning - crowned not by the world, but by your own Divine remembering.

And as we rise, one by one, the collective crown shines brighter - illuminating a new era of conscious, sovereign, radiant womanhood.

This is not the end. This is the Sacred transition. This is *Herstory*, finally being written, through you, through me, through us all. The story I've shared here is not just mine. It is **our** story, Herstory - every woman who has walked through her own fire, every Heart that has broken open under the weight of transformation.

I bring you this story now because it matters, but because WE matter. Our voices and choices matter.

May this chapter serve as both her-story, a mirror, and a map. A mirror to remind you of your own brilliance, and a map to guide you through the fire toward your inner diamond. Women need to read the map: the days of nothingness that precede the dawn, the small, steady practices that rescue the nervous system, the food and supplements that act as allies, the threshold of the thymus as a gateway. We need to know that sovereignty is not simply a thought but a steady practice of tending.

Allow your mind to rest in the knowledge that initiation is not the absence of pain but the making of you into something brave and luminous. You are not alone. The lineage remembers you. The Crown is not lost - it is waiting to be recognised and claimed by you.

And I am here to serve you, woman in Menopause, to alchemise the shitstorm into Soul alignment.

Thank you for reading my "shitstorm", my story. <3

## Women I'm Inspired By

I am inspired by my mother, from Finland, who in this small, tiny body she has a strong "sisu" which is Finnish and freely translated means "never give up". She was taking care of my father in his final months of life, and after his death 2024, she has gained her energy, motivation and zest of life back.

I am also inspired by my own Daughter *Livia*. She is a young woman, only 20 years but super creative, with a strong will, and a voice of an Angel. Her name means "Life" in Swedish- and she has so much life force in her body, so it is almost crazy. She is one of my biggest Teachers in Life. Her communication skills and big Heart inspire me. A lot.

# Reflections

# Reflections

# In Closing

There is a temptation, when looking back at history, to believe certain women, like the ones listed below, were exceptional. That they had some rare quality the rest of us lack. That their courage was born in them whole. But that is the easy story, the comforting one. The harder truth is this: they were ordinary women who refused to accept the limits placed upon them.

Nawal El Saadawi, Wangari Maathai, Bibi Khanum Astarabadi. Harriet Tubman, Mary Prince, and Mary Seacole. Queen Amanirenas, Khadija bint Khuwaylid, Ada Lovelace, and Chien-Shiung Wu. Frida Kahlo, Aminatta Forna, Olufunmilayo Ransome-Kuti, Mariam al-Asturlabi. Helen Keller, bell hooks, Yayoi Kusama, Betty Campbell, Ada Blackjack. Doris Lessing, Harriet Jacobs, Madam C. J. Walker, Ilhan Omar, Coco Chanel, Ayn Rand. Ann Burgess, Leila Khaled, Elif Shafak, Vandana Shiva.

Their names alone are an education as very few of them are recognised by the majority of women around the world, and yet their courage is what has made the lives women today lead possible. Their lives are a rebuke to every excuse we have ever made.

Each one of them stood in the face of ridicule, violence, or erasure. Each one of them carried on. Some wielded words, others marched with thousands, others worked quietly, inventing and solving complex problems the history books failed to mention. Some planted trees, some painted their bodies into art, some navigated ships by stars, some wrote memoirs that tore the veil off a nation's conscience. They all walked different paths, experienced different pains and frustrations, but underneath it was the very same refusal to give up.

What humbles me is not just what they achieved, but what they endured to do so: Prison, exile, poverty, illness, ridicule. To be told again and again: no, you do not belong here. And yet, here they are in records which are now coming to light. They are now in our memory and in the very soil we walk upon.

Being a tree hugger, I am in awe of the fact that Wangari Maathai planted trees as acts of rebellion, and they are still standing. That Harriet Tubman crossed marshes at night with people who trusted her with their lives. Ada Blackjack survived the Arctic alone because she had no choice. That bell hooks made love a political weapon. Queen Amanirenas fought Rome and forced peace on her own terms. That Khadija bint Khuwaylid built an empire before anyone thought it possible.

What binds them is not glamour, or luck, or even brilliance, though they had plenty of all three. It is their grit, vision, and an unshakable refusal to stay silent.

It is humbling to admit that most of us will never know the level of risk they lived with daily. Yet here we are, beneficiaries of their choices, with the inventions and freedoms they created, creating nothing more than excuses. We read freely because others were imprisoned for writing. We walked into classrooms, failing to remember that women were, and still are, barred from education. We organise, we speak, we vote, we plant, we create, all because someone before us refused to obey the system, the patriarchy and the doubts within them telling them they couldn't.

So what do we do with our inheritance? Admiration alone is not enough. Awe, if it stays private, is a kind of theft. To honour them means to pick up the tools they left us with, words, art, courage, strategy, and solidarity, and we put them to work. We get to rise up against our fatigue, we get to choose to silence the nay-sayers in society

- and often within our own families. We get to choose every day to be the very best version of self, leaving our excuses at the door. Why? Because little girls and boys, and other women, are watching, needing role models to look up to.

This chapter does not end with their names by accident. It ends with them because every page of this book belongs to their company. Their legacies are the foundations we are building upon, they are the beginnings, the invitations, and the demands for us to own our power, own our ovaries - the very centre of creation for life itself.

And so I leave you with this:
Carry their courage into your own battles, however small they may feel.
Refuse the silences that keep injustice safe.
Plant something real.
Write something true.
Build something that outlives you.
Do it with humility.
Do it with awe.
Do it because history is calling, and now it has called your name.

As women, we have the power to create, grow and give birth to life, and if we can do that, we can do anything!

# Book Club & Women's Networking Group Questions

## 1. Medical Negligence and Bias

1. Have you ever had your pain or symptoms dismissed by a doctor, and what effect did that have on your confidence and trust in your own body?
2. Why do you think women's pain continues to be minimised or misdiagnosed, even in supposedly modern societies?
3. How does race, class, or sexuality influence the quality of healthcare women receive?
4. What would accountability look like in a medical system that routinely fails women, and what would need to change?
5. How can women begin to reclaim authority over their own health when the system is still steeped in bias and neglect?

## 2. Patriarchy and Power

1. What does "owning your ovaries" mean to you, and how does it challenge traditional ideas about femininity and strength?
2. Where do you see patriarchy operating in your daily life, in institutions, language, or relationships?
3. Why do some women continue to protect patriarchal systems, even when they're harmed by them?

4. Do you believe the modern feminist movement has lost its clarity of purpose, and how might we reclaim it?
5. How do we teach our sons and daughters about equality in a way that honours both biology and humanity?

## 3. Violence Against Women and Girls

1. Which story in *Owning Our Ovaries* struck you most deeply in its portrayal of abuse or control, and why?
2. How do we as women protect sacred female-only spaces without descending into fear or factionalism?
3. What are your reflections on Sal Grover's case in Australia, and how do you see the erosion of women's spaces affecting women's safety?
4. How can collective storytelling serve as a tool for breaking cycles of silence and shame around violence?
5. What does genuine safety look like emotionally, physically, and socially, for women today?

## 4. Career, Financial Freedom, and Sovereignty

1. How has financial dependence or independence shaped your choices in relationships, parenting, or health?
2. What does true financial sovereignty mean to you, beyond pay rises or promotions?
3. How do societal expectations of women as carers and nurturers impact our professional aspirations?
4. When have you held yourself back from stepping into power or visibility for fear of backlash or judgment?
5. What changes would make workplaces genuinely inclusive and empowering for women, not just performatively so?

## 5. Cultural and Generational Issues

1. How has your cultural background influenced the way you see womanhood, family, and freedom?
2. What generational patterns of silence, shame, or submission are you breaking in your own life?
3. How can women from different cultures stand in solidarity without erasing one another's lived realities?

4. What lessons can we draw from the women throughout history who fought, spoke out, and died for our rights?
5. Will the women of today show the same courage, strength, and resilience as those who came before, and what would that look like in action?

## 6. Honouring Your Ovaries

1. What is your relationship to your ovaries, and what do they mean to you?
2. How much time do you spend thinking about or connecting to your ovaries?
3. If you knew how much information the ovaries store, not only from this lifetime, but from many reincarnations, what would that mean to you?
4. What would be possible for you if you deepened your connection with your ovaries?
5. How are you going to connect on a deeper level with your ovaries from now on?

# Journalling Prompts

We invite you to contemplate the following journaling prompts below to help you gain more from the stories shared and your own journey through life thus far.

- I own my ovaries by...
- I have been dismissed or silenced by medical professionals when...
- I now recognise that my pain was not weakness, it was...
- I was told "nothing is wrong" when in truth...
- The moment I realised I had to advocate for my own body was when...
- I have lost trust in the healthcare system because...
- I am learning to trust my body again by...
- I have internalised medical bias by believing...
- The words I wish a doctor had said to me are...
- I will no longer downplay my symptoms because...
- I honour the women who were experimented on or ignored by...
- I am reclaiming my health story by...
- I will teach my daughters (and sons) that women's pain is...
- I have every right to ask questions, demand answers, and say no because...
- I see now that silence around women's health serves...
- I am redefining strength as...
- My healing begins when I...
- I forgive myself for trusting those who failed to see me because...

- I am part of a generation of women who will no longer...
- My ovaries are not a metaphor; they are my reminder that life, wisdom, and power begin within me. With this knowledge, I am going to ....

# Gratitude

Thank you to all the ladies who have so kindly gifted their stories for this book in the hope that other women may be inspired, encouraged and know they are not alone in this world. I know it has not been easy to write and share your stories, and the courage you have shown by doing so leaves me humbled and incredibly grateful to you all.

To all the ladies who said they would be part of it and are no longer, I thank you for the lessons you taught me. They were not easy lessons to learn, but you showed me on so very many levels that when someone shows you who they are, believe them.

Thank you to Amanda for the incredible illustration you created after we discussed my ideas and concepts for the artwork, and to Jerry for bringing the ideas, illustration and concept altogether with your design magic.

And to my sons, Khaalid and Naasir, you are the reasons I get out of bed on my most challenging days to write, create and show up. Without your ongoing support, love, encouragement and unwavering belief in me, I would not have achieved half of what I have achieved. I write to show you that what you think, feel and believe is important. Never let anyone silence you. Always believe in yourself and learn from my many mistakes. Together we can achieve greatness for ourselves, for others and for those to come. I love you.

# About the Publisher

DBI specialises in publishing impactful literature on the human condition, social justice, exposés, anthropology, and cultural cohesion. Our books aim to create positive, lasting change and provoke thought and powerful discourse, inspiring readers to see the world through a more conscious and empowered lens.

While we often publish non-fiction, we also publish fiction. Our non-fiction includes memoirs, autobiographies, and anthologies with up to ten contributors. We also welcome ethnographies, creative non-fiction, and selected works that amplify marginalised voices. Our fiction range is one which challenges beliefs and ideas, whilst celebrating relationships with self and others, and amplifying political or cultural narratives.

Our authors are dedicated individuals committed to creating high-quality, influential works, ready to invest the time, effort, and resources necessary to make a significant impact. We support our authors in navigating the publishing process authentically and confidently. DBI works closely with an international team of experts to help our writers share their stories genuinely.

Founded by Dawn Bates, an award-winning, international bestselling author with a global reach spanning five continents, DBI is grounded in experience, expertise, and a fierce commitment to social change. Dawn's background as a leader, entrepreneur, activist, and world traveller enables her to coach writers with insight, guiding them to embrace their unique voice and navigate the journey to becoming a published author.

In addition to publishing, Dawn serves as a biographical writer, researcher, and developmental editor, as well as an exceptional author coach, supporting writers who work with agents and other publishers.

DBI also offers thorough manuscript assessments, which include basic copy editing, marketing strategies, and suggestions for brand expansion and creating additional revenue streams. These assessments are designed to equip authors for the realities of publishing and build a successful career beyond the initial release.

To learn more about DBI, visit https://dawnbates.com

www.ingramcontent.com/pod-product-compliance
Lightning Source LLC
Chambersburg PA
CBHW070040230426
43661CB00034B/1451/J